HIS
STUBBORN
LOVE

HIS STUBBORN LOVE

A DRAMATIC ACCOUNT OF A YOUNG COUPLE WHO ALMOST LOST THEIR MARRIAGE

JOYCE LANDORF

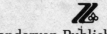

Zondervan Publishing House
Grand Rapids, Michigan

© 1971 by Zondervan Publishing House
Grand Rapids, Michigan

Zondervan Publishing House,
1415 Lake Drive, S.E.,
Grand Rapids, Michigan 49506

ISBN 0-310-27122-3

Library of Congress Catalog Card Number 70-133355

Grateful acknowledgment is made to:

Holt, Rinehart & Winston, Inc., for lines from "The Road Not Taken"
by Robert Frost, from *The Poetry of Robert Frost,* edited by
Edward Connery Lathem.

King's Business magazine for "Thou Shalt Not Kill" by Edith Wyvell.

Lockman Foundation for passages from *The Amplified New Testament.* © 1958 by Lockman Foundation. Used by permission.

Unless otherwise indicated, Scripture passages are from *Living New
Testament* and *Living Psalms and Proverbs* © 1967 by Tyndale
House, Publishers, Wheaton, Illinois, and are used by permission.

Printed in the United States of America

85   86   87   88   89   /   35   34   33   32

*When I asked her if she ever thought I'd write
a book, she smiled and said, "I always knew."
Since she left us too quickly, please tell her,
dear Lord, the book she "always knew" I'd write
is dedicated to her, my mother,*
MARION UZON MILLER

ACKNOWLEDGMENTS

No one, I repeat, no one, ever sits down and writes a book "all by myself." Oh, I know there are those weeks, months, and sometimes years that a writer disappears from society and hibernates with his typewriter, but even then he knows he's not really writing alone; and if by some lovely plan his book is published, it's going to happen because of a lot of other people. In my case, people come in two distinct classes: IDEA people and TIME people. If I named them all, the acknowledgment pages would exceed the book pages, so I'll name only a few, but rest assured there were many more.

IDEA PEOPLE

These are the people who by their suggestions, books, ideas, or letters have spun me around and shoved me toward writing. Al Sanders gave me the first nudge by asking me to write for *King's Business* magazine. Those writings caught the eye of Floyd Thatcher and then Pat Zondervan, head of the Zondervan Publishing House. Then there was a host of other *Idea* people like my pastor, Dr. Edward B. Cole, who has molded many of the thoughts of this book by his consistently preaching what God would have him say. Every writer is influenced and inspired by other writers. The ones who have made the biggest impression on me are writers like Dr. Henry Brandt, Dr. Tim La Haye, Keith Miller, Henrietta Mears, and Dale Evans Rogers.

Spanning the gap between *Idea* and *Time* people is one young man, Chuck Leviton. It was Chuck who walked into the dark rooms of my soul, grabbed my hand, and pulled me into God's marvelous world. This world of flashing sunshine and brilliant hues of color continues, even now, to dazzle me with amazement and wonder. It was Chuck who looked at me and saw what God had in mind.

TIME PEOPLE

These are people who, by giving of their love, encouragement, and time, kept me from losing hope and from chalking the whole thing up as a gigantic mistake. With an incredible investment of their understanding and time, these dear ones pushed, prodded, and pulled me up the long, steep climb. I'm everlastingly glad they did — the view from here is breathtaking!

No one can estimate how much a family gives so one can write, and my debt to my very dear husband and precious children can never be paid in money. Even my parents, in-laws, and relatives had their share, and sometimes I only saw them on Christmas. Oh, bless their big hearts!

Finally there is a whole host of friends and co-workers who laid aside goodly portions of their life to write through my pen. How do you ever thank such people? (Don Brandt, pastor of the Lincoln Ave. Community Reformed Church, and his marvelous wife, Perky; Ruth and Rollin Calkin of First Baptist in Pomona; praying friends like Eleanor Moore, Charlotte Edwards, Pat Zondervan, and Conn and Clare Bauers.)

The military term "aide-de-camp" sums up my feelings about these last-to-be-mentioned-but-not-least-in-appreciation people.

Richard and Virginia Smith, who spent an incalculable amount of hours tidying up my unsystematic way of writing.

Ginger Luber, who in the very early days of writing began volunteering her typing ability and did the first drafts, and finally, Sheila Rapp, my dear secretary who, in great love, polished off the final manuscript and managed a steady stream of love and encouragement with each page.

Every author knows these people are the real writers of any book, and I'm personally grateful to them all.

PROLOGUE

"Lord, lead me as You promised me You would;
otherwise my enemies will conquer me. Tell me
clearly what to do, which way to turn.
For You bless the godly man, O Lord; You protect
him with Your shield of love."   Psalm 5:8, 12

Less than a month ago, at this writing, my husband Dick
was nearly killed twice within two hours.

It had been a quiet evening. Our family had eaten dinner
together, and then Dick left for his banking class; Laurie,
then thirteen years old, completed her homework assign-
ments; our fifteen-year-old son, Rick, after having skied his
way into a broken ankle, was spending most of the evening
figuring out how to get comfortable; and I caught up on
some extra mail from my radio broadcast.

Later that evening, after Laurie was in bed, I helped
Rick in and out of the bathtub (no easy task) and we both
had come unglued with laughter as we coped with the
ridiculous situation. As I was busy bedding him down, the
time seemed to slip away from me, and not until I heard
the phone ring did I absentmindedly look at my watch and
think, *Who would be calling me at 11:00 P.M.?* and at
the same moment I casually wondered why Dick was an
hour or so late.

The voice on the phone was strangely familiar, yet distant and slightly blurred. "Honey, I'm all right, I'm all

right. It's me, Dick. I'm all right . . . please don't panic
. . . I'm all right."

After he told me he was all right five more times, I knew
the rather irrational voice belonged to my husband; he was
in desperate trouble, and he was NOT all right.

Dick's night had been anything but quiet, and what
started out as a routine evening at a banking class ended
in a frightening nightmare.

First his small foreign car suddenly spun out of control
on the wet slippery pavement that rainy evening. After his
car hit the freeway divider fence, he awoke to find himself
hanging out of the car with an upside-down view of the
approaching cars. Even in the drizzling rain, with his
glasses gone, bleeding from his nose and mouth, and his
head almost on the pavement, he could dimly see and hear
the oncoming cars. They were honking, blinking their
lights, and slowing down.

His first impulse was to run, and with slow, painful
maneuvering, he struggled out of the car. However, once
out on the pavement he changed his mind and decided to
see if the car would start. Amazingly, it did, and he drove
with a rather blind sense of direction to the side of the
road.

Without his glasses, his visibility was about three or four
feet, but by squinting his eyes he could dimly see a white
sedan that had pulled up onto the center divider strip.

By now he was bleeding profusely, cars were blinking
their lights, and traffic was moving cautiously around him.
Finally a man asked if he could help. My husband remembers an enormous flood of relief as he thought, "Thank
God, the Highway Patrol."

The man's face loomed into focus in front of Dick, but

he was not dressed in a police uniform; rather, he wore a heavy sweater over a sport shirt, blue jeans, and his breath reeked of alcohol as he asked if Dick needed help.

Dick answered, "Yes . . . just get me home. I live a few miles down the freeway — or take me to a phone so I can call my wife — or to the hospital — I do need help."

The man ran back to his car, the same white sedan Dick had seen before, and said something to two men who were still seated in it. He then returned to our car, pulled both left fenders away from the tires, helped Dick into the passenger seat, started the car, and asked for directions. Dick in detail, told him the way to our home.

Just two miles down the freeway, however, the man took the wrong exit. By now blood was pouring out of Dick's mouth and a massive headache had begun. He had lost one front tooth and had sustained multiple cuts and bruises on the face (later we learned he had two concussions). In spite of all this, he sensed that they had turned at the wrong place.

"What are you doing? Where are you going? Please take me home," he pleaded.

"I've got to talk with my two friends in the other car," the man explained. While he was gone, the swelling began from Dick's eyes down to his mouth, and the pain and confusion became unbearable. He was glad the man returned, but was confused again when they didn't go back to the freeway. The car headed south.

"I don't live down this way," Dick said thickly.

"I thought you couldn't see where we're goin'," the man stated.

"I can't see too well, but I can tell by the lights and signs we are going *away* from my home." Then an incredible thought occurred to him, and he formed the equally incredible question into words: "Are you kidnapping me?"

"Yep," the stranger said matter-of-factly.

When the impact of the answer finally registered, Dick knew it was too late to jump out, for by that time they were driving along a dark country road.

After some time, the two cars found their way to a deserted section of land, a wooded sloping hillside some twenty-five miles from our home. The man told Dick to get out.

"Are you going to rob me?" Dick asked from behind his blood-soaked handkerchief.

"Yep," came the unruffled answer.

In the darkness Dick could faintly see the man's sedan parked a few yards behind him and could make out the shapes of the other two men. One man stayed in the car the whole time, but the second, a small man (actually the fourteen-year-old stepson of the man robbing Dick), got out, and walked over to the car beside Dick.

The first man began his systematic search for valuables, taking everything from Dick's wedding ring to his wallet and bank keys. He knew what he was doing and accomplished his search quickly and professionally. When he found only two dollars in the wallet, his composure was shattered and he grew furious with rage. "Is that all you got?" he screamed.

Because of a great blood loss and a state of shock, the general confusion that followed isn't too clear in Dick's memory, but it seemed there was an argument between the man and the boy about what they would do with Dick and how soon he'd go to the police. It was the boy who demanded that Dick be "taken care of" because "he's gonna go to the cops right away."

Dick was sure they planned to murder him, so he tried to divert their thoughts by pleading, "Please leave me my keys." Then as he bartered for more time, the man hesitated a moment, had a change of heart, and finally consented and put the keys in the ignition. It was the boy's turn to be furious, and he made the man take the keys back. The boy then lifted up the hood, pulled all the wires from the motor, broke everything that was left to break, and in his anger would have worked Dick over (possibly killing him) had it not been for the protecting hand of God.

After he took the spare tire and had left Dick lying face down in the front seat of his car, the man and his "helpers" jumped into their car and roared away into the darkness.

How Dick ever got out of that area without running into trees, stumbling into boulders, or falling over logs we will never know, yet somehow God's hand guided him to the road and he ran towards a distant light. It was a porch light, and he kept running until he reached the house.

Dick pounded on the door, and finally a man opened the little peep hole, took one horrified look at the grotesque, bloody face outside, and kept the door firmly closed. Dick kept knocking and pleading to enter, and after a few minutes the man changed his mind.

"Thank God you opened the door," Dick said.

It was stated in such a reverent tone that the man quickly looked up and said, "You're a Christian!"

"Yes, I am," murmured Dick.

"So am I," responded the man.

We will always be grateful to him for his Christ-like help and concern that awful evening. The man first tried to lessen the swelling on Dick's face with cold cloths; next he called the police, and then he called me. After Dick told me briefly where he was, the man carefully spelled out directions to find his home.

While Dick waited for me to get there, his host tried to relieve his shock and physical pain by quoting some psalms and verses of comfort.

Back at our home I replaced the phone receiver and a wave of panic started surging over me, yet I knew I had several things to do and now was simply not the time to go to pieces. Trying to remain calm, I told Rick what had happened and then phoned a neighbor to come and stay with the children.

At first, I thought I would drive to Dick alone, but then I realized in my present state of mind I could easily miss a turn-off so I called the first of several friends. No one was home. The panic renewed itself with vigor. I swallowed hard, put my hand on the top of the phone directory, pulled myself together, and breathed, "Lord, You know I need someone to go with me; I can't find this place alone, so please direct me to someone who is close by and still up." (It was almost midnight!)

Then I opened the directory, and the first name I saw was that of one of the ministers at our church, Rev. Keith Korstjens, who lived only a few blocks away. He answered before the first ring had stopped.

"Keith, are you still up and dressed?"

"Yes, Joyce, what's wrong?"

"I need you. Dick has had an accident, been kidnapped, robbed, and is out past Chino. I have to go and get him."

Without further conversation Keith said, "I'll be right there."

When we reached the house sometime later, I jumped out of the car and began running up the steep steps to the porch above me. Through the drizzling rain I could see two men. One of them sounded and looked a little like Dick, but I couldn't understand the hysteria in his voice as he shouted, "Who's down there? Who are you? Who's there?"

"Honey, it's me; it's Joyce," I said as I got closer and knew it was Dick.

"Who is that with you? Who is it?" he demanded before I could answer. His tone was one of desperate pleading now.

"Hon, it's Keith. It's all right," I said as calmly as possible.

When I reached him, my mind could not believe what my eyes clearly told me. I recognized him by the coat he was wearing. The red blood pouring from his nose and the ugly black swelling around the eyes and cheeks were monstrous.

All I could think was, "Oh, darling, what have they done to you?" Dick was looking past me and staring closely at Keith.

Finally he said, "I thought you were one of the men, that you had taken Joyce as a hostage and were coming back for me." As it turned out, Keith's car was almost identical to that of the kidnapper.

On the drive home, Dick couldn't seem to grasp the idea that he was safe. He said incoherent things and his speech was impaired by the enormous swelling.

When we reached home, Rick was up and fully dressed. With his leg in a cast, I'm still not sure how he managed. The mother in me functioned perfectly, and typically I said, "Why aren't you in bed?"

"I don't want to miss anything," he said simply. Laurie slept peacefully through the whole thing.

Soon our house was bursting at the seams with police and sheriff's deputies. In the midst of all this confusion, our family doctor came, recommended oral surgery later that day, handed me a large sedative to give Dick, and then he wrote the longest, most involved case history on record. Just before he left he said, "I've seen it, but I don't believe it!" We couldn't believe it either, but at least we knew it was true. The results of the crime were all too evident. At least they were to me and to Dick, but we were alone in this conviction, and one of the most intriguing aspects of the whole incident was one we would have never foreseen. The authorities did not believe Dick. Slowly it dawned on us that no one, aside from our minister and doctor, put one ounce of credibility in Dick's story.

"It's too difficult to believe," said one sheriff.

"There are too many odd factors," said another.

Not one policeman or sheriff wrote down a list of stolen articles. They just kept asking the same questions all the time. "How much have you had to drink?"

"I don't drink."

"Where were you earlier this evening?"

"At a banking class."

And in the middle of this I was thoroughly startled when I heard the sergeant say, "Okay, sir, let's go."

Before I could grasp the meaning of his statement, Dick, still holding his ice pack, was pulling on his overcoat.

"Where are you going? Where are you taking him?" I gasped.

"Don't worry ma'am, we'll bring him right back." Now, that line *really* reassured me.

I still find this part hard to accept, yet on that dreadful rainy night, still suffering terribly, Dick left with the sheriff's deputies and they retraced the actual route from the accident to the robbery site. Then they took him to the sheriff's station and over and over Dick repeated the story. But even then, as he waited for them to return him to our house, a new sheriff walked in and asked the man at the desk, "Who's that over there?"

The officer at the desk gave a slight laugh and said, "He says his name is R. E. Landorf, but who knows?"

It was almost four in the morning when they dumped Dick out of the squad car in front of our house after questioning. When I let him in, he just stood in the hall and wept. "They don't believe me. They don't believe me" he sobbed. We then barricaded the door, and I phoned our local police to ask for protection during the night. They were very polite but treated me like some kind of little old lady in tennis shoes and declined my request. I couldn't convince Dick to take the sedative the doctor had left because he knew there really were three men out there somewhere who knew exactly where we lived and were in possession of all our keys. Our safety was at stake.

I had been married to Dick for sixteen years and knew his character and brand of truthfulness. I knew if he had said there were thirty men out there with our possessions and our front door key, it would have been true! The more we tried to make sense of the events, the worse the situation became. I felt like we were living in some foreign country and were experiencing all the horrors of a police state.

We finally climbed into our bed stiff with fear. Once I

quoted, aloud, Romans 8:28, and twice after that we said it together, but the fear froze and paralyzed us anyway.

Back at the sheriff's office, they were having a busy night, but just before dawn a young deputy who had been working on several cases besides ours took a good look at our case on the clip board. The clip had obscured Dick's name, so idly the young man pulled the sheet down to read the complete report. Suddenly he raced into the sergeant's office and quickly blurted out, "If that's the R. E. Landorf that taught my Sunday school class when I was in high school, we've made a mistake about him. He's telling the truth, and if he says there are three men — *there are.*"

At that very moment the stillness of our bedroom was shattered by the ringing of our phone. Dick had the phone in his hand in a flash.

"Yes, yes, it is, I'm R. E. Landorf. Yes, I did, except I didn't lose those credit cards; they were stolen tonight . . . you do? Where? Thank you, I'll call too." Then he dialed the sheriff's number.

"The motel clerk at the Holiday Inn says the three men are there. They used my credit card."

The sheriff's deputies were at the motel within minutes, and the young deputy who had been in our Sunday school class made the arrest just as the three men were getting into their car to leave the area.

One newspaper account ran a headline that said SAMAR-ITANS STRIP MAN OF VALUABLES, and part of that story ran like this:

> A Pomona man said he was robbed Tuesday night by three men who stopped to help him when his car hit a free-way fence.

The good Samaritans later used his credit cards to buy two tires and rent a motel room, sheriff deputies said.

The motel clerk, however, became suspicious of the many telephone calls the men were making. He called the credit card firm for the address of Landorf. When the clerk reached Landorf at home, the victim called the sheriff's office.

Deputies said they reached the motel just as the three men were leaving. They arrested all three on charges of strong-arm robbery and kidnapping. (*Daily Report*, Ontario, California, February 14, 1968.)

As we look back on that terrifying night, we know God spared Dick's life twice within two hours: once at the accident scene and once at the hands of the men. Out of this experience evolved an intensified concept of what really matters in life and what, at best, is only trivial. I once again realized that my elegant marble-topped coffee table was not worth a cent to me unless Dick had his feet on it, and that the pretty rose dishes my mother left me were not precious unless my whole family was eating together at mealtime.

I found, too, with a new awareness, that God's hand follows His children much like the space-age tracking stations follow the flight of the astronauts, and no detail is too small or too obscure to escape His computer-like attention.

When I think of what God has done for us in the past ten years, I find it as incredible to believe as the details of my husband's kidnapping, yet I have watched God keep track of us all these years, spare our lives time and time again, and with great love give to us the abundant life He promised.

Not long ago I was singing for a Sunday school rally, and after my first group of songs, the assistant minister came forward to give the opening prayer. I must confess I did not hear any of his prayer past the first ten words, as he abruptly interrupted my thoughts by saying, "Oh, God, thank You for Your stubborn love towards us."

I'd never heard anybody refer to God's love as "stubborn," and suddenly I realized I was sitting in that church, alive, well, and singing as God had intended, simply because of HIS STUBBORN LOVE. And before I sang my second group of numbers, I knew I had the title for this book.

HIS STUBBORN LOVE . . . His very stubborn love towards us has always been the most tenacious love, although for a time Dick and I were so caught up in ourselves we didn't notice it, but it never discouraged God as He doggedly pursued us.

This is our story —a true story — a story about His penetrating, persevering, stubborn love and its miraculous, dynamic force in our lives.

HIS
STUBBORN
LOVE

1

"Our children too shall serve Him, for they shall hear from us about the wonders of the Lord."

Psalm 22:30

I think I have ALWAYS been in church. Since I was born, I have been in church. No, before I was born I was in church. My mother took about three days out of church life for my birth, and then I was right back in church! There were Tuesday board meetings (no babysitters in those days, so I went WITH mother) which alternated with ladies' meetings, Wednesday prayer meetings, Thursday choir rehearsals, Friday church potluck suppers, and Saturdays to clean and prepare for the really big day, Sunday. *That* day started with a fast breakfast at 8:00 A.M., Sunday school at 8:30 (we always got there early), church at 11:00, home for dinner at 1:30 (nobody quit preaching at noon), back to church 5:00 P.M. for young people's services, and finally to the 7:30 evening service which drew its final breath around 10:45 P.M. In fact, by the time I was seven, I had been sitting in church so much I was suffering from a spinal condition called "rump-sprung."

It wasn't that my parents were religious fanatics. It was simply because my dad was a minister. My early life was suspended in the church and I was surrounded by Christians. We had Christian friends, Christian relatives, Christian fun, and Christian activities. In those early days, to be surrounded by this Christian life was a warm, wonderful experience. My young memories are filled with love and laughter. For example, there was a lady in our church in Owen Sound, Ontario, Canada, who tithed her delicious hot rolls because of a limited income. Each Saturday I asked God to keep Mrs. Evers financially poor so she'd continue to tithe hot rolls to the pastor. As a child of seven, I was thoroughly convinced that God had honored my request (one of my first) because the rolls kept coming the three years we were in Canada.

About that same time, I learned about my father's Irish sense of humor. Actually it had been there all the time, but I had not been old enough to appreciate it. He could always ward off a childhood tragedy with a squeaking noise he made with his mouth or an impromptu melody on his invisible trombone. (Occasionally it was a tune on his other invisible instruments: an Hawaiian guitar or a Jew's harp.)

Playing a trombone that was real was one thing, but playing one that didn't exist was *extremely* difficult. Yet by putting his mouth a certain way, he could play a most sparkling, triple-tongue, slide trombone arrangement on any song the occasion required. Whatever he lacked in money and material things, he made up for in good humor.

My Uncle Pete still talks about the time he visited my mother and father shortly after my birth. The church was paying my father a ripe, round salary of three dollars a week, and they had very little food, clothing, or furniture. But Pete still reminisces about the delicious food he ate (my mother whipped it up out of nothing . . . a talent I've

28

never mastered), the darling dress she was wearing (she rescued it from the missionary barrel and added trim and buttons), the fantastic dresser and end tables made out of orange crates (she found them behind the market, bought some remnant chintz, and turned them into decorator pieces), and her marvelous way of looking at life.

It's no wonder that I loved her so much and wanted to be just like her. It was no wonder, either, that at her side one Sunday night when I was seven, I asked God to come into my heart, exactly as I had been taught by her. I simply had always loved God and had always known He created me, so taking Him into my heart was a natural step. Besides, as my mother had often reminded me, "You must be the example; you're the minister's daughter."

I shall not mention our church or our denomination by name, only to say that many churches of that time and place held similar theological concepts. I was not a theologian, but I was intensely aware of the rigid rules of the church. There were long lists of things you could not do, could not use, and could not see, and much shorter lists of what you COULD do or what God could do through you. I was not sure who set up the lists, but I always felt it must have been some man who had a terrible childhood involving his mother. It was obvious he had not cared much for women, because a lot of the rules and sermons had to do with how women dressed, evil "lip rouge," and gossiping. As I think of it now, there were more sermons on "lip rouge" than on gossiping.

The negativism and legalistic views of our church were difficult for me to understand as a child, and my father's delightful sense of humor seemed far more removed from all the strict, forbidding rules of the church. I could never seem to gain a perspective or balance about the two. For instance, why was it such a sin to wear a red dress when God created such red, red roses? Why were so many sermons preached condemning radio (later it was television) when most of the ministers and missionaries I knew had radios?

I began looking at Christians and non-Christians, and the comparisons that were forming in my mind were alarming.

It seemed that somewhere, lurking in the back of my mind, was a huge chasm with high bluffs on each side. Standing on one side of the bluff were my dear parents, and on the other side were the nauseating "church-going Christians." The chasm between was unbelievably deep, and the two groups of people seemed to have nothing in common.

This chasm was characterized by a Christian lady in my father's church who never ever smiled. I'd known her for a long, long time and had *never* seen her smile. I felt that if she ever did smile, her face would crack into a hundred pieces. She also was always the first one up at Wednesday night prayer meeting to give the same stone-cold, rut-deep testimony. It went: "I have known the Lord for thirty years, and I have the JOY of the Lord down in my heart." She used to scare the socks right off me because of the ice in her voice and her stern-set jaw. I would think, "Boy, she really does have the joy of the Lord down in her heart . . . WAY down!" My dad had been preaching the "good news of Christ," and yet she looked as though she had heard nothing but bad news all her life!

Then there was the business of "all those hypocrites" in the church . . . and I must say, no age group catches on to hypocrisy faster than the teen-agers. As a teen-ager I could never understand how one particular man in our congregation could pray all those wonderful prayers on Sunday morning and yell and rave at his kids like a madman on Sunday afternoon. He was really rare during their family devotions.

Once when I had been invited for dinner and witnessed his "performance" as a father, I thought I'd split with wonder. This happened when, after dinner, he yelled at the top of his voice, "All right, you blasted kids, sit down and shut up . . . we're gonna read from the Bible." As far as I could see, the announcement was not met with too much eagerness. I marked it down in the secret place of my heart as an excellent example of hypocrisy at its zenith. This man's life was an obvious mass of contradictions, and my father spent a great deal of time counseling with his wife, his children, and businessmen who had been cheated by him.

Another lady in our church completed my thesis on Christians. She was one who could never say anything without quoting (or rather misquoting) Scripture, generally taking it completely out of context. I can still recall how subtly she impressed us with her spirituality by relating how long she prayed, how early she had gotten up to do it, and how much Scripture she had memorized. In fact, she was so busy memorizing Scripture, she didn't have time to talk to her neighbor, which was a real pity, for the neighbor needed a friend desperately. Whenever dad asked her to help in Sunday school, vacation Bible school, or in women's missionary meetings, she was always too busy — we never did find out at what. Yet her favorite line was "Now, pastor, if you need anything done, just let me know." That line was used just slightly less than her other favorite which she handed my father at the door of the church after each message, "Well, pastor, that was a fairly good sermon, but I think you should have quoted from Job, chapter three, and you possibly could have tied in Matthew 2:12." I always wondered what kind of a fabulous preacher my father could have been if this lady would have spent as much time praying for him as she did in criticizing him.

Once when I entered the church vestibule, my arm was hurting and I was rubbing it. This same lady was the only one there and I said, "Oooh, my arm hurts right here."

Scripturally up to the occasion, she piously said, "If thy right hand offend thee, pluck it off."

The look I gave her was probably the same expression I see today on the faces of teen-agers as they ask, "What are you, some kinda nut?" This lady was some kind of weird, old nut who couldn't even say "hello" without throwing in some Bible verse.

I wondered if when I grew to be an adult Christian, I would end up wearing many-sided masks like the man I'd observed, or would I turn out to be a hopelessly incurable, weird, old lady, warped and twisted by a phony, hypocritical tourniquet called Christianity?

By now I was really taking a long, hard look at Christians, and what I was seeing began stretching into one puzzling and unbelievable picture. The chasm was widening between my wonderful Christian parents, loving and serving God with quiet sacrifice and great joy, and the church with its lists of "don'ts," its lack of joy, its hypocrites, and its share of religious nuts and fanatics.

Was this some kind of huge joke God had played on the world, or was it a rather pathetic and accurate picture of the church and Christians at large? By now I had seen thirteen years of a pastor's life within the church, and, to put it mildly, I was pretty disillusioned with its people, its ministers, and missionaries, as well as its total purpose.

In September of my thirteenth year, my parents sent me some four hundred miles away to a Christian academy. My first evening in a dorm was not what I had expected. I had envisioned Bible reading and dorm prayers and had really looked forward to meeting young, honest Christians. I even hoped that some of my nagging questions about God could be answered. Actually that night we spent about a half an hour in the act of washing nylons (School rule #1: wear nylons *always*. I'd never worn a pair, much less washed any,) and about three hours listening to our senior roommate describe her sex life in glorious, living detail. It was, at the very least, an eye-opening evening.

Three semesters in the Christian academy thoroughly convinced me I'd never make it as a Christian, and I was fairly sure I would never make it as anything else either. All it took to convince me I'd be a failure was a student voice teacher who less than tactfully told me to give up singing as I just wasn't physically built for it. I wondered how I had won the Michigan State Youth Award in the eighth grade for singing if I wasn't built for it.

The legalistic, narrow, negative rules once more bound my heart and spirit, and I established within myself a very basic rule of my own: I would have no part of this repulsive, phony, negative Christianity. I'd far rather be a sweet but honest pagan.

While my mind and emotions wanted to be a sweet pagan, my heart had been raised in another direction, so I made some lukewarm commitments to God, rather general, but commitments nevertheless.

As a minister's daughter, I had seen hundreds of people go to the altar and give their hearts to Jesus, and I knew I would take this step someday as well as I knew which fork to use and when to say "please" and "thank you." It was part of my home training. Many children accept Christ at a very young age, and it is a real born-again experience; but with me, it was a brush with God — logical and sincere, but very casual. It was done in the same manner that I memorized Scripture and songs and the books of the Bible, done because it was expected of me. Early in my life I learned two distinct languages; English and the language of the church. I spoke both fluently.

The major commitment occurred when the blossoming of my singing voice was called to my attention by a public school teacher. (Just the year before I went to the Christian Academy.) She had been trying out voices for girls' glee club, and as she listened to the high sopranos, she asked if anyone could sing higher than (she touched the piano) a certain note. I hummed and rather timidly raised my hand. Later, after a few more notes, she asked me to come up, and while I stood by the piano she played past high C, D, got to E, and made this breathless announcement: "Class, someday you and I are going to say with pride, 'I knew Joyce when she was in school' because she is *very* talented and has a *great* voice."

I was very impressed and fairly flew home to break the news to mother. "Mother, mother, I am going to be a great singer. . ."

She was stirring something on the stove, and she turned and looked at me, kept stirring, and said, "That's nice, dear, now go practice your piano." Mothers: the great even-uppers!

However, I did begin to seriously study voice at the Detroit Institute of Music. Soon many people in my father's church began suggesting that it would be wonderful if I would give my voice to God. This commitment seemed to be the right thing to do, exactly as I had been taught, so, just before I left for the academy, I proudly marched down to the altar and "gave my voice to God." (Big deal!) The dramatic effect, especially on the older folks, was effective and complete. I really wowed them.

Even as I made this commitment, I was slipping on the robe of rebellion, and while it was long and heavy, I liked the feel of it. But I know now that a rebellion, while it *may* start in a marvelous, adventuresome, and thrilling way, *always* ends in the opposite direction. For what was marvelous turns to bitterness, what was exciting and adventuresome becomes boring and unsatisfying, and what was once thrilling turns out to be an experience in anguish, ending in the most despairing kind of defeat and humiliation. How do I know? Oh, I know because I have experienced the despair of the damned, and I have graduated from the school of rebellion.

What I thought would be my sweet, marvelous, adventuresome rebellion began simply enough. Nothing earth-shakingly bad, no great sins, just a general statement of fact when I looked directly at my mother and said, "Mother, you don't have to worry about me committing all kinds of horrible sins or even about smoking, drinking, and not being 'good,' but there is one thing I've decided I do *not* want to be, and that's a Christian." Mother did not shock easily; I do not remember even a flutter of eyelids, but she saw clearly my new shining robe of rebellion.

From there I began to plan a deliberate life strategy:

1. I would be good, sweet, and charming at all costs. (Play-acting and masks would be the order of every day.)
2. I would go to church. (Especially when they asked me to sing.)
3. I would be kind and sweet to my parents and older people. (It generally paid off.)
4. I would attend and join various Christian youth activities. (Basing my choice on such important matters as who was in the group, what boys belonged, and where my music would be a stepping-stone.)
5. I would remember in the depths of my inner heart exactly what phonies Christians really were, and I would live my life as I saw fit. (In effect, I ordered, "God, You stay up there and I'll stay down here. You leave me alone, and I'll not bother You, and we'll *both* be happier.")

Looking back . . .

We have always had rebellion, especially in the young, but having lived through this terrifying, honest-to-goodness rebellion, I have no idea as to when it overtook me. I thought *I* was having a rebellion, but somewhere, early in the experience, it changed. Instead of being a robe or some wild, new cloak I'd put on, it reconstructed itself into a vine, a small but poisonous vine, rooting itself in my heart and beginning to grow. It was fed by the church, my Christian academy experience, and hypocritical Christians. It was watered by my own belief that God simply did not care.

There are hypocrites everywhere, but why is it we always notice them in the church? Shyster lawyers, quack doctors, lying salesmen — all hypocrites, but I suppose the world hopes that at least in the church they won't find them. We quickly forget the church is made up of imperfect people — people just like you and me. My pastor has often said, "If you do find a perfect church, free of hypocrites, and you join it, it will no longer be perfect."

Oh, how we love to use hypocritical Christians and a Christian academy, as I did, as an excuse for the way *we* live and for the decisions *we* make. If we could only realize that when a person is a religious hypocrite, it tells us only what *he* is, nothing about the nature of God; but unfortunately, we respond much faster to excuses than to personal honesty.

A writer once wrote that after God created us, He flung us to earth and went back to heaven to sit in His rocking chair and watch the messes we got ourselves in and out of. After I saw firsthand the messes a lot of Christians found themselves in, I was pretty sure this was an accurate picture of God. A God who did not care about us once He had created us, so why bother serving or loving Him?

The tenacious tentacles of the vine squeezed spirit and breath from me and blinded my soul to the fact that God would spend many years *out* of the rocking chair, tirelessly and tenderly proving His stubborn love for me — a love laced with ribbons of steel, strong and binding. I was yet to learn that the song I knew from my childhood, "His Eye Is on the Sparrow," would, one day, unfold to me the side of God's personality that showed *how* He cared for me. He would not only prove all of this to me, but for years

He would prune, sometimes gently, other times ruthlessly, the monstrous, hideous vine of rebellion until my soul was completely unbound and free. He would also, each morning of my life, awaken my heart in quick wonder because of the knowledge that even before the beginning of time, He had cared — *Oh, how He had cared!*

2

"But the Lord is still in His holy temple; He still
rules from heaven. He closely watches everything
that happens here on earth."   Psalm 11:4

My singing voice led me to the man who eventually was
to share my anguishing rebellion and suffer from it too.

One night at a youth choir rehearsal, in the middle of my
solo, in walked a handsome, blond, blue-eyed collegian
named Dick Landorf. It had rained all day, and I was
hiding my limp, straight hair under an old scarf. I'll never
know what Dick saw in me, but he turned to a friend (later,
our best man) and whispered, "See that girl? Well, she's
the kind of girl I'd like to marry."

A year later, when I was seventeen, I bounced into my
mother's bedroom, swinging Dick's high school ring on a
chain, and with a great flourish said, "Mother, I'm going to
marry Dick Landorf." Had I told her I was going to ride in
a parade as Lady Godiva, I couldn't have created a more
traumatic moment. Contrary to all scientific laws, I'm sure
the world stopped twirling for the next few moments.

Her icy response was, "Dick *who?*"

After the feathers and fur stopped flying and things had
calmed down a bit, I assured her I had no intentions of
marrying him *immediately*, but someday, when I did marry,

it would be he. As all mothers do, she had picked out several candidates, and she was terribly disappointed.

As I think back on it now, all of her sensible objections to our marrying were quite valid. "It would take a miracle to make you two compatible," she said. (That's *exactly* what it did take.)

She went on to point out that Dick's background and family life were totally different from mine. His parents had been divorced when he was about ten, and he had lived with his father. She also called to my attention, "He doesn't have much musical talent or ability." (She really had her heart set on a concert pianist named Everett.) My defense about his lack of musical aptitude was that we had met in choir. She reminded me that the fact we met in a choir did not mean Dick was musical; it only pointed out that nearly *anybody* can sing. In the end, I explained all her objections away by stating the age-old reason lovers have used, "But mother, we *love* each other."

I graduated from high school and during the next two years of junior college, I studied all the marriage courses possible, pored over all the brides' books and magazines. I dreamed as any nineteen-year-old girl would about the day I'd become Dick's bride.

The music department kept me busy outside of school representing the music division and inside with at least ten productions plus a senior recital. I was singing secular music with school productions and sacred (gospel) music at church, youth rallies, and Christian musicals like Phil Kerr's regular Monday Night Musicals in Pasadena.

Schooling, part-time working, singing, voice lessons, and three years of dating Dick finally brought our wedding day into reality. Dick had completed his Army training and one year in the Counter-Intelligence Corps and had been assigned to the Los Angeles area. I was a wise twenty-year-old and Dick an even wiser twenty-three, so all was set.

June fifth came, and four bridesmaids, groomsmen, matron-of-honor, my brother as ring bearer, hundreds of guests, gifts, and many lavender flowers later, we were married.

The marriage was storybookish in setting and feeling. It seemed, from the beautiful white chantilly lace gown to the delicious Hungarian pastries served at the reception, that the prince and princess would probably live happily ever after. They would live and love in their own castle, tending their own affairs, raising their own children; and to other people in their kingdom, they would be charming, helpful, and understanding.

The princess had a few doubts in the midst of that wedding day, but who doesn't? So, she brushed them aside. Now she had the prince she loved, and what *more* could she ever need?

Looking back . . .

When I talk with teen-agers today, they often voice this same thought. "Love," they tell me, "will somehow, some way figure out all the problems." I wish this was realistically and statistically true, but in the everyday press of marriage, your educational level, your religious heritage, your cultural attitudes, your economic status, and your racial traditions all become major concerns. Somehow, there is just not enough love to go around. The pressures of family, peers, and society seem to crush out the love in a slow but sure way. Furthermore, what, besides experience alone, can tell you how it is to look at each other every morning, 365 days

41

consecutively, for better or worse, in sickness and in health? That's what the nitty gritty of marriage is all about; that day in, day out living. Love, out of physical and surface attraction, or even out of companionship or arrangement, is not enough to keep a marriage glued together. But love, involving two people who are secure in their relationship with God, the Author of all love, welds a unit so strong it can ride out any storm. Their marriage will hold together during any earthquake and, after fifty years of marriage, reflect that a precious love in the beginning has become even more precious as each day, each year has passed. That kind of love affair is *only* a miracle of God's stubborn love!

3

"Everyone deceives and flatters and lies. There is
no sincerity left."   Psalm 12:2

The lid on the box of memories for the first year of our
marriage is very hard, even now, to pry off. Perhaps it's
because there were no flashing red light warning signals
to predict the scalding horror of future years; no bold, clear-
cut incidences, major confrontations, or rebellious truthfulness; just a fuzzy, blurred picture that shaped itself on my
inner thoughts before I was awake in predawn hours. I
remember a vague discontentment — nothing really serious,
but rather a nebulous sense of impending sadness. Since we
were in love, I had only to reach out to Dick, be surrounded
in his arms, and feel his need of me to push the fears into
the farthest corners of my mind.

I have no way of remembering just when it was during
the first year that simply lying in Dick's arms was not
enough. Somehow the vagueness of the discontentment had
now shaped itself into words . . . actually into questions.

*Is this REALLY all there is to marriage? What WERE
all those shining girlhood dreams of being a bride, a wife,
a woman, and where were they now?* I could scarcely remember.

I suppose the first crack in the barely hardened glue that held us together happened just a few weeks after we were married.

Dick had received his Army orders that stationed him at the Presidio in San Francisco, California, so we lived for three or four weeks with Dick's delightful, cosmopolitan, truly San Franciscan Aunt Louise. She adored Dick but had an instant LOVE for me. I suspect it was because of our mutual love for music. It was about the very essence of music that Dick and I had our first serious honeymoon disagreement.

Aunt Louise and Dick went to their jobs each day, and I puttered around in auntie's house, played her piano, read some books from her vast library, and eagerly awaited their homecoming each night.

Most every evening after dinner (we were on Army pay and couldn't afford an evening out) the three of us sat and talked, until one night Aunt Louise decided she would have me teach her everything I knew about music (she could master anything she touched).

Dick, a new bridegroom, naturally wanted my full attention. Aunt Louise, a frustrated musician, wanted her house filled with as much music as possible. I didn't exactly ignore Dick during those evenings, but I adored his aunt's eager questions and receptive mind, so I played, sang, and taught for hours on end. None of this pleased Dick, and I, who had been raised with music, could not understand his selfish attitude.

"After all, we'll only be with her a few weeks," I reasoned with Dick. "Why not give her music to her heart's content?"

Dick's sullen ultimatum came stinging back, "But I want

all of you, all of your time, and I don't want you to spend the evening at the piano with her!"

Had I been wiser or more mature this tricky issue probably could have been worked out, but music was so much a god to me that I had no intention of giving up or even slowing it down, so I continued playing and singing. Aunt Louise became happier; Dick became cold and withdrawn.

I was caught in the middle with my love for Dick on one side, my love for music on the other.

Dick was quite pleased when his orders arrived and we were transferred from San Francisco to Los Angeles.

The first of many conflicts over music was eased and smoothed over by the hustle and bustle of moving into our first apartment. I took a job in a toy store to occupy my daytime hours and augment our Army pay, but the dinner hour each night began our second conflict.

It seemed quite evident that I really could not cook, and what was worse, I had little or no desire to learn how. Playing the piano and singing was much more suited to my temperment.

Cooking might not have been such a disaster except that Dick felt divinely inspired to "help" me. He had his way (the *right way*) to do everything. I had a masters degree in the *wrong way* approach. Mention veal cutlets to Dick today and his mouth breaks into a marvelous grin. Mention them to me and I'll cry!

Actually, all the domestic aspects of marriage were quite beyond me. Once during that first year, to impress my relatives, I served a dinner for twelve. Spareribs and sauerkraut. Everything went fairly well except I forgot to put the spareribs into the oven. By turning the heat way up, postponing dinner forty-five minutes, and apologizing every sixty seconds for the tough, underdone ribs, it was truly an unforgettable evening. Whatever I lacked in culinary ability, I made up for with sheer nerve.

Shopping for food, cooking it, cleaning up afterward, paying the bills, and keeping a house clean were all areas of my life I faced with a blank stare. Oh, I tried all right, but you could say I wasn't too gifted in the home economics department. I'm not sure how I got WORSE at cooking and cleaning, but I managed it.

We were no more settled in our darling apartment when my father accepted a call to a church in Barstow, California. They lived a few blocks from us in a fifty-year-old house which I had always loved. It didn't take much talking to convince us to move into it.

Both Dick and I enjoyed the burst of activity in moving, cleaning, wallpapering, and redoing, so much so that we didn't have time to concentrate on differences, conflicts, or my cooking. (I read once that one of the tendencies of neurotic women is to continually redecorate — I think I know the problem and understand the reasoning. It's a great escape method.)

Our joint efforts in that big, sprawling California house were rewarded by the praise of our families and friends. The house was lovely when we finished. Its spacious living-room, family-sized dining room, three bedrooms, kitchen, breakfast room, and high-ceilinged bathroom were somewhat big and overwhelming for just the two of us, but after the Landorfs bought us a bedroom set and my folks a baby grand piano (both delayed wedding presents), we really began housekeeping — light housekeeping.

Once the flurry of activity stopped, however, old conflicts warmed and rose to the surface, and music became the thorny irritant in our daily living. How something so beautiful, important, and necessary as music could bring on so many arguments was simply beyond me!

Phil Kerr, the song writer, was holding Monday night musicals, and I had been one of his regulars since I'd been sixteen. The concerts were made unique because of Phil's on-stage ability to move and warm audiences and his off-stage ability to inspire and encourage artists and young musicians. Singing on the Pasadena Civic stage to 3,000 people was one of the most priceless musical educations one could ever have.

Before we were married those musicals gave Dick and me the exciting pleasure of dating, meeting fabulous musicians, and eating out afterwards with Phil and top musicians, pastors, and "greats" in the Gospel field of church music. I soaked it in and stored all the learning I could take.

After marriage everything changed. At least, as far as Dick's attitude everything changed, and as he pointed out: first, we didn't need to date anymore; secondly, he was sure the *only* reason I wanted to sing at the musicals was for the applause; thirdly, since he was not a musician, he found my musical friends slightly egocentric and practically weird.

For the second time in one year I was again caught in the middle over music. On one hand was Phil Kerr offering me the opportunity to perform before thousands of people, and on the other my husband who wanted me to stay at home with him. I'm sure this conflict was neither new nor unique with musicians, and over the years I've watched more than one marriage dissolve over these same problems.

During that first year of marriage I made the mistake of playing the piano for a while after our evening meal, something I had always done at home. Dick took it for several months, and then one night in a stern, but controlled voice he said, "Joyce, I wish you'd stop playing the piano each night so I can enjoy the music on the hi-fi set."

I remember the night so vividly it still hurts a little. Never in my twenty years of living had anybody asked me to STOP playing the piano — except once or twice when I was a little girl and my mother wanted me to stop stalling and get the dishes done.

I remember thinking, *He doesn't want me to sing at Phil Kerr's musicals . . . he doesn't like my musical friends . . . he resents my going to church choir practice because it takes me away from him . . . and now he wants me to stop playing the piano when he's around. What have I gotten into — what have I married?*

In my parents' home, if I wasn't singing or playing, my dad was. If he wasn't, my mother was. If she wasn't, visiting ministers, missionaries, or young people were giving their latest song a go-around. In some homes the big, round, dining room table was the center hub of family living, but in our household it was definitely the piano. Now I was being asked to consider a home without piano playing.

I didn't know it then, but adjusting to the kind of marriage Dick wanted would be a task that eventually would tear my spirit into shreds. A marriage with little or no music and a lot of domestic activity began to emerge, and I felt the first imperceptible touch of panic.

Our first wedding anniversary came and went that warm June, and even though I was definitely against (rebelling is a more accurate word) being a wife and "housewife," my joy at learning I was to be a mother pushed all drudgery away. Like millions of women before me, I had high hopes that a child (particularly a son) would ease the growing tension between Dick and me and give more direction to our lives. The baby would be the glue to hold us together. As the months passed, I began piling all my hopes and dreams in that baby's bassinet. I was *so sure* it would work.

The birth of our son, Rick, was quite routine; that is, it was as routine as one can be if it's the first, three weeks early, with a husband away in San Francisco getting his Army discharge, and only three hours of labor for a warning.

The minute the nurse brought my baby around the delivery table, he opened one of his beautiful blue eyes, looked at me, and there began a love affair that's still going strong. Five days later Dick arrived from San Francisco. The nurses fixed my hair, helped me into a pale blue negligee, and then ushered Dick in to see me. Whatever rebellion I'd felt toward our marriage melted away when he said, "Oh, Joyce, you look so beautiful." The tender hope nurtured in that reunion was the only glimpse God allowed us to feel, because before too many months had passed, the rebellion had returned — only stronger and in another part of our marriage.

Each night it was the same routine. Dick would come home, say a brief "hi" to me, peck me on the cheek, and ask, "Well, now, where's my son?" While I was pleased with his devotion and playtime with our son, it was easy to figure out exactly what *my* role was. It boiled down to this: clean the house, keep the baby bathed and fed, and feed and make love to my husband (not necessarily in that order). I didn't feel needed as a person; it was more like a refrigerator or stove-type need. "A very useful appliance, that's me," I thought, "but who wants to be an appliance?" I could foresee wearing out and being replaced by a newer model.

One morning after we had been married about two-and-a-half years, I looked up at my handsome, blond, blue-eyed husband and said, "Ugh," or words to that effect. "Why in the world," I wondered, "did I ever choose you?" Dick, I knew looked down at his vivacious brunette and said, "Ugh," right back, meaning essentially the same thing. Here we were, two reasonably attractive, intelligent people with an absolutely beautiful baby son, the right job, the right neighborhood, the right number of cars in the garage, the right number of dollars in the bank, and both of us were totally miserable and disillusioned with the whole mess called marriage.

Actually, there were two sets of us. One set was the charming couple: they were nice neighbors, friends, and relatives. They acted out their roles as husband and wife in sugar-coated politeness.

The other set was the two people who took the happy masks off once the front door had closed and pursued the acid honesty which was eating away their marriage.

In our third year of marriage our little girl, Laurie, was born. In spite of her RH condition and two emergency blood exchanges, she fought for the right to live and succeeded against tremendous odds. She was, and still is, a beautiful blue-eyed blond. She was, and still is, as feminine and petite as Rick is masculine and strong. Our love for our children knew no bounds, and yet the miracle we had hoped for in our marriage had not occurred, even with Laurie's birth.

Laurie was over a week old and still in the hospital when a speeding ambulance raced me back to the hospital and into the antiseptic operating room. I had hemorrhaged almost to the point of no return.

Earlier that morning, as I waited for my parents to arrive (mother was to stay a week and take care of things), the phone had rung and I had bounced up quickly to answer it. Immediately heavy hemorrhaging began. I stumbled back to bed, and the most incredulous thoughts glimmered on the horizon of my mind. They were strangely calm, deliberate, and contemplative thoughts, and they formed quickly.

I guess mother couldn't get away from the house. They are so late . . .

The rate of hemorrhaging is increasing . . .

I should call the doctor, but if I don't call him and the folks don't get here soon, I could slip into shock, or maybe a coma, and then just die very neatly and quietly . . .

It would be suicide . . .

No, it would be an accidental death to everybody but me; I'd know, but it would be such a welcome relief to die . . .

My thoughts ended abruptly when I opened my eyes and heard my mother say, "Dad, she needs an ambulance right now!"

Maybe, I thought, during that frantic race to the hospital, *I'll die in surgery. It would be so good to be free from all the masks.* I almost got my wish that day, but try as I might, I couldn't die.

That day marked the first of many death wishes which

were to come. What had been merely frustrations in marriage now took on the first signs of depression. In the weeks that followed, I finally returned to my role as wife, mother, and housekeeper and did the usual horrid job in all three areas.

"I always got D's in home economics classes and in sewing, so what could anyone expect?" I rationalized.

It was then that I read some pretty enlightening books written by some very sharp girls. They said over and over again, if you had any brains at all (I felt I did) or talent (oh, yes, that was me), you should get out of the house and fulfill yourself. *Fulfill yourself!* These words were facing me everywhere, and they took hold in fertile soil; I began to see a glimmer of hope — a way out. All I really needed was to *be fulfilled*.

How? Ah . . . education. Yes, that was the answer. I auditioned with a renowned teacher of secular singing in Hollywood, and to my delighted surprise was accepted as her student. Yet, as time went on, I felt I was learning nothing, so I quit and chalked it up as another defeat. I then enrolled in a distinguished and famous school of drama. I had the sneaky little feeling that if I could just get to the top of my class, my dreams for fulfillment would be a reality and it might make an important change in our marriage. When I did reach the top of the class, I came home bursting with visions of stardom and announced, "Dick, I've graduated top in my class; isn't that just marvelous?"

Barely looking up from his paper he said, "Mumm, that's nice, dear; by the way, do you have a shirt ironed for me?" His words covered me with a familiar, icy-wet blanket.

There I stood, all decked out in my new fulfillment, and his reaction was complete indifference.

As a matter of fact, the word "fulfillment" had lost something in translation, for *never* before had I felt so empty. I could see that education was no answer, at least not for me, so what was left?

Looking back . . .

I think we all wear masks. Even Christians. If you don't believe me, watch the next time someone says, "Hi, how are you today?" And even though the washer broke down in the middle of a load, the baby has a terrible diaper rash, and your head is simply splitting, you smile and tell the lie, "Why, I'm just fine, thank you." A counselor once told me he spends the first forty-five minutes of an hour session getting the person to take off the mask, and only the last fifteen minutes is spent finding and discussing the real problem.

We wear our masks well. This is why, as concerned Christians, we should never look at a person and decide for ourselves whether he knows Christ or not. Judging others may be pretty dangerous because some have had considerable experience at wearing masks. I think I could have fooled you, as I fooled my parents, relatives, friends, and neighbors, for my mask was firmly in place.

4

"O Lord, have mercy on me in my anguish. My eyes are red from weeping; my health is broken from sorrow. I am pining away with grief; my years are shortened, drained away because of sadness. My sins have sapped my strength; I stoop with sorrow and with shame."   Psalm 31:9, 10

In the fourth year of our marriage I realized with a dreaded finality that nobody — NOBODY ever tells brides about all those dirty dishes and real housekeeping. I must have heard hundreds of lectures on marriage and had a thousand thoughts on the subject, but none of them ever included coping with the soiled laundry or the ever-present mountain of dirty dishes (except in unrealistic soap commercials on television).

We've all heard about the drudgery of being a housewife. Some women changed the word to "homemaker," hoping that retitling it would somehow help, but it certainly didn't for me.

Along with the frustrations of all those dishes and diapers, something else was added; Dick and I were no longer talking to each other. Oh, there were the same tired generalizations about what cute thing Rick had said or whether it was raining early this year, but all of it was small talk —

no genuine communication. We never discussed the goals for our marriage, the ever-changing goals of our children, or our personal heartfelt needs, desires, and ever-present fears. No, only small, very small talk.

With the small talk came large silences. The house was wrapped in an atmosphere of cold silence, and lying deep in the core of that silence were two rebellious hearts and two unforgiving spirits.

Ordinarily, rather routine conversations took on double meanings. Dick's "Good morning" took on sarcastic overtones that sounded like, "It's certainly nice you finally rolled out of bed to fix my breakfast." And in my "How would you like your eggs?" you could plainly hear, "You'd better not give me any special instructions, because you're mighty lucky I'm even up."

I am convinced the silent war we waged wreaked havoc on our children, and most of the bitter exchanges between us were duly recorded by the two little minds. In the fourth and fifth years of marriage, the children had broken arms, collarbones, and concussions galore. I didn't realize it when it was happening, but I feel certain now that those accidents were not accidents at all, but a chain reaction to the bitterness that chilled our household. Being accident prone was not confined to the children either, as I burned myself on the stove frequently, and rarely did I *ever* cut anything up without cutting myself too. Dick had a scientifically impossible (yet real) case of the flu each morning for two to three hours. I'd tell him unsympathetically that he had no temperature, but he would relate how he ached all over and sometimes he actually vomited. He would force himself to go to work, but looked forward to the weekend when he would crawl into bed and stay there. I got slightly tired (to put it mildly) of this routine, and I suggested he snap out of it, develop a sense of humor, and try to get back to normal. He was so different from the man I had married. It never occurred to me to look in the mirror. I wonder if I *had* looked if I would have seen the fantastic changes that had twisted my face and personality.

We kept up the silent cold war which was warmed only by the fires of rebellion deep within our hearts. What had started as a marvelous, adventurous rebellion was now a sonnet to loneliness.

I tightened the chin strap on all my masks, tried to ignore my loneliness, and plunged downward to a new, insane depth of despair.

Insane is the right word, too, because along with wearing our masks and arranging silent wars, Dick and I played little married-people games, subtly at first, but later with great vengeance. "Who's in Charge Here?" was the name of one game. Sometimes it was my turn to be "it," and other times, but less frequently, it was Dick's turn.

One of the rules in this little game was, "since I'm going to be boss, don't tell ME what to do!" It was quite ridiculous actually; here we were each vying for the "boss" position but not speaking to each other in the process. It's easy to see the glaring frustrations of that game.

My husband began learning about temperamental, Hungarian-Irish people like me, while I began learning about stubborn, neat Germans like him. Dick ignored my admonitions about "don't tell me what to do" and regularly mentioned my lack of neatness. As his "telling" sessions became more and more frequent, I became more and more irritated. To myself I thought, *Well, thank you loads, Mister Clean,* but being a nice, civilized girl, I smiled and sweetly answered, "Thank you, Dick, for your suggestions." I discovered it's perfectly possible to smile and grit your teeth at the same time.

Being neat is not too bad until you are married to someone whose neatness equals your messiness. If your husband is as neat as mine and you are as messy as I am, then you already *know* he fastidiously rolls up the toothpaste tube and *never* forgets to replace the cap. You, on the other hand, rush in, remove the cap, squeeze it as hard as you can (dead center), and leave off the cap. This, of course, sets up the morning argument which probably means a ruined breakfast, an agitated ulcer, and a high-tension headache.

Dick superintended my every move; once when he came into the kitchen while I was pulling open (destroying) a bag of potato chips, he offered this suggestion: "Darling (actually his tone of voice said, 'Hey, Stupid'), the potato chip company has spent millions of dollars scientifically sealing this bag so that all you have to do to open it is tear off a corner, slit it, and it's done very neatly."

I thought, *Just once, Herr Commandant, I'd like you to talk to me without it sounding like a Gestapo order.* Then, there was the day he told me how superior his mother's pot roast was to mine. When he proceeded to give me step-by-step directions, I listened, smiled artificially, and thought, *You tell me how to do one more thing, and you and I have had it. We will be finished!* He didn't disappoint me.

The "big, important" issue that brought all our masks and games out in the open involved one of the most mundane items in the entire house: a roll of toilet tissue!

Dick called me into our bathroom, pointed to the roll, and said, "You've got this on the *wrong* way." It sounded like I had committed a horrible ax murder.

I thought, *He's got to be kidding. He's not serious.*

He went on to say, "You've got the paper towels in the kitchen going the wrong way too."

I managed to make a shocked, squeaking noise and said, "It doesn't make any difference!" But it did make a difference to Dick. The roll had to be hung with the paper rolling off the top and not hanging down the wall.

All of this led to an emotional discussion of why it *did* matter. We both discovered we'd been switching rolls for years, each thinking the children were turning them around. Somewhere in the middle of it all I heard him say, " . . . and furthermore, I can't live in a house where it's going the wrong way!"

"That's just FINE with me," I screamed at the top of my lungs.

One argument and four hours later there was nothing left of our lives, our marriage, or our home. Piece by piece we had destroyed one another. There were no walls now, nothing was left standing, and two people's lives had been flattened out as if a giant steam iron had simply pressed them out of existence.

I always wanted to melt, mold, and shape that neat German into my designs, but I only succeeded in breaking him into smithereens. Standing there that afternoon, I saw the final disastrous results of my work. I had, indeed, cut him to my specifications, broken him in mind, and stripped him of all his masculine dignity. I flogged him with my inadequacies, my neurotic temperament, and all my failures. When I was finished, there was nothing left of him. I was shocked and sickened at what I had done, but by then it was far too late.

It was all over . . . gone and buried . . . and I felt exactly as if I were walking from a newly turned grave. I was sure I was losing my mind, and in the madness of the moment I knew I had married the wrong man. There could never be any purpose to life, especially in the area of music, and I now certainly knew no one cared about me, nor understood. The first two things I could probably learn to live around, but the third thought was overwhelming, and it began a new era in my life. The era of no hope.

Looking back. . . .

Even now I ask, Oh, God, when did it all start . . . this seething resentment toward anyone, anywhere telling me what to do? How do you differentiate between just innocently wanting your own way and the deep sin of self and rebellion?

I believe it starts in all of us as soon as we are born. The Bible states clearly, "All have sinned. . . ." That fact is obvious even in a child before he is a year or two old. If you need conclusive evidence, try telling your little darling it's time to take his nap. Ask him if he wants to go beddy-bye, and even though he can hardly talk, he becomes multilingual and says "No" in six different languages. He's really telling you, in no uncertain terms, you are NOT to

59

tell him what to do. This baby grows into a junior-higher, and one day he comes home, slams his books down, and blasts out, "Who does that history teacher think she is, giving me five pages of homework?" The tone of his voice reeks with "don't tell me what to do." Then he gets his first job and soon you hear, "Well, if HE thinks I'M going to take that from HIM, he's crazy." When marriage comes to this young man, we find him shaking his finger at his wife while he lays down a ground rule for this marriage. "Don't you *dare* tell me what to do." Of course, the whole thing finalizes when this man looks up into the face of God, shakes his tiny fist, stamps his little feet, and hysterically screams, "God, don't you tell me what to do."

How clearly I see myself here: so definitely rebellious, so careful to do everything exactly as I wanted, making my own decisions, forming my own opinions, and insolently thrusting my little clenched fist into the face of God.

How small and insignificant the roll of toilet tissue seems now, but so often it is not a big crisis that destroys a marriage. It is the simple, everyday things. How well I can identify!

C. S. Lewis wrote in his book, *The Great Divorce*, "there are two kinds of people: those who say to God, 'Thy will be done,' and those to whom God says, 'All right then, have it your way.'"

The moment had come in our marriage when God loosened His hold on us and said, "Have it your way." He did not let us go completely; He just gave us a little slack on the rope. So we lived together one more year, not as husband and wife, but as two separate people, hanging over the cliff with precious little rope left.

In the month of May, a few weeks before our fifth wedding anniversary, a familiar thought danced across my mind. *I'd rather be dead than celebrate a 'happy' anniversary.* The thought grew bigger each day, and finally it consumed all my waking hours. One day it abruptly turned into a question, *Why should I live another second?*

5

"Death bound me with chains, and the floods of
ungodliness mounted a massive attack against me.
Trapped and helpless, I struggled against the ropes
that drew me on to death.
In my distress I screamed to the Lord for His help.
And He heard me from heaven; my cry reached
His ears."   Psalm 18:4-6

Each morning the pattern became the same: the shrill in-
terruption of the alarm, the first stirrings of Dick by my
side, and a desperate wish to keep on sleeping. Each night
it was a herculean effort to get my extremely tense body
relaxed enough to fall asleep, so when the moment of awak-
ening arrived, I longed to stay asleep, as if I could somehow
escape all the frantic jumble of problems just by slipping
my head under the covers. It seemed, too, that no matter
how long I slept, I was always fighting total exhaustion —
fatigue was my constant companion.

One morning as the routine pattern was about to begin,
I forced myself to consciousness, dragged my feet out of the
covers, and dejectedly contemplated the dreary day ahead.
As I sat on the edge of the bed, I caught sight of my feet.
They were chalky, death-white in color, and they made

quite a contrasting sight with the brilliant red throw rug just under them. I stared down at them for some time and then quietly thought, *My feet look so dead . . . why put them on the floor? Why get up at all today? Why live? WHY LIVE?*

As the day dragged on, the question burned into my brain. Finally, about one in the afternoon, when the children were outside, I calmly made up my mind. Almost in a trance I thought, *I'll be free from this horrid world forever.* I had no idea the "peaceful calm" I was experiencing was the eye of a hurricane that would soon break me apart with all its fury.

Devoid of emotion, I deliberately made my way through the house and into the bathroom. There, like a sleepwalker, I opened the medicine chest, found the razor blades, and methodically began unwrapping a new package. For a split second my parents' faces flashed before me, and I could see with great clarity their grief-stricken, disappointed eyes. Mentally I pleaded with them to understand that this was the only way out.

I lowered the blade to my left wrist.

Before the razor touched my skin, the stillness of the house was shattered by the shrill ringing of the phone. I stood still, listening, and then automatically began counting the rings.

Five, six, seven . . .

I thought, *How dare anyone interrupt me, especially now!*

Ten, eleven . . .

Why don't they hang up?

Thirteen, fourteen, fifteen . . .

I wondered what could be so important. I felt, however, that nothing, no matter how important, could alter or change my decision. The persistence of the ringing finally angered me so much I ran into the bedroom, yanked the receiver to my ear, and shouted, "Hello."

It was a man I had met months before, a minister and a fairly casual acquaintance.

Now he was quietly talking to me. The anger in my tone must have been obvious, but in his gentle manner he was saying, "I don't know what you are doing right now, Joyce, but whatever it is, stop it and listen to me."

I thought, *Oh, no, that's all I need — a minister! I* was in no mood for religion. Didn't he know I needed neither him nor the Bible? Didn't he remember *who* I was? If I'd wanted a minister, I'd have called my dad.

Suddenly, I became aware of what he was saying. True to form, he was quoting from Scripture, but because the words were so contemporary and the sentence structure so understandable, I could barely believe it was from the Bible. It certainly wasn't the King James Version, and as the words continued, I felt compelled to listen.

"Don't be vague, but firmly grasp what you know to be the will of God." He emphasized the words, "What you KNOW to be." I was so caught up in those words that I missed the next few lines he read but heard him finish with, "Having done all, stand firmly in place."

Stand firm? What did he really know about my life, my marriage, or my failures? Slamming the phone down, I stalked back to the bathroom.

I stopped in front of the mirror and then gasped in disbelief. I'd never seen the woman before me. She was old, sick, neurotic. She couldn't have been more than twenty-five, but her rebellion had shriveled her face up into ugliness; it sagged with the dried, leathery look of the aged. The lines around her eyes were hard-set in anger, the pinched look about her mouth twitched with nervous worry, her voice level had been preset to "whine" because of the "poor-little-old-me" attitude, and her exaggerated make-up and way-out hairdo added a sad-comic-clown feeling, making the whole face hard, yet pathetic. Worst of all, however, was the vacant nothingness in her eyes.

Standing there before the mirror that day and seeing myself, I could only say, "Is that woman me?"

It was then that the enormity of the phone call began to hit me. The timing was so perfect, the voice so quiet and thoughtful, and those words, oh, those words!

Those words would not leave me alone. In the stillness I heard again, "Grasp firmly what you *know* to be the will of God." I looked up at the newly painted white ceiling, "Oh, dear God, what *is* Your will?" Then a chilling thought sliced through me, *Do You even have a will or plan for me?*

Then, from the depths of my memory—like some long forgotten dream — came the verse: "The Son of man is come to seek and to save that which was lost." The last word, *lost*, thundered over me like the breakers in the Pacific Ocean surf! *Lost, that's me, Joyce Landorf. That's my middle name.* Aloud I said, "I am lost in every direction. Lost as a wife, lost as a mother, as a cook, a housewife, and most of all, lost as a human being.

For a moment one glimmer of hope seemed to shine through. Could it be that God cared for me after all? The old wave of darkness quickly closed in again as I reasoned that even if God *did* care for me, it was sheer insanity to ever think He'd forgive all my ugly sin and rebellion. He WAS God and all that jazz, but He wasn't THAT great. After all, I'd had five years of gentle sinning before marriage and five years of down-to-business sinning after marriage, and I didn't see how anybody could wipe that kind of slate clean.

An often-quoted verse ended my thoughts, "If we confess our sins, he is faithful and just to forgive us our sins, and to cleanse us from all unrighteousness." My mind seemed to skip the forgiving part, and I thought about the cleaning. "Oh, God, do I need a cleaning." I wondered if God knew just how much cleaning it was going to take. When I did get around to thinking about the forgiveness of God, my only worry was — COULD God forgive me? I was to learn it would be much more difficult for me to forgive myself and it would take much longer.

Then, I thought, *What else did he say? The part about "stand firmly?" Could that be the clear unmistakable voice of God saying, "do not use that razor"?* My back stiffened with a growing awareness of the actual presence of God and a wave of fear swept over me.

I fled from the bathroom to the living room and dropped to my knees in front of a green wingbacked chair. As I looked down at the cushioned fabric in that big chair, I dazedly began to see my whole life spread out before me like a detailed map. The map started with the tracing of all the goodness God had given me in my parents, my younger brother Cliff, and little sister Marilyn — those precious people I had never learned to know and love.

I vividly remembered Christians like the one who said, "If the church young people want to go roller skating, it's all right, but the preacher's daughter shouldn't be seen in such a place." And as I remembered, I recognized a fantastic bitterness in my own heart. It came as somewhat of a shock because I had always prided myself on my unbiased and just opinions. Funny, too, all the years of my bitterness never touched those hypocritical Christians in any way, but oh, what disaster they brought me.

Then, leaning over that chair, I began to see clearly all my own selfish attitudes and my sheer conceit about "my" talents as they marched there before me in a long, disgusting parade. I have no idea how long I knelt there that afternoon, but the big map with its roadblocks and detours seemed to unfold for hours. I saw, besides the past, the present outline of my life. Dick, the children, my resentments, depressions, and uncontrollable temper — all of it was there. I stared at my life as if it were the very first time I'd ever seen it. I was acutely aware that I was not looking through my own jaundiced eyes, but, in a limited way, through the eyes of God as He must have seen my life from His perspective. For the first time, I felt the full heavy weight of my ugly sin. God's view was unlike anything I had ever fathomed. When you *are* able to take a good look at yourself as *God* sees you, then, and only then do you begin to understand why just "thinking good thoughts" or "trying to be good" is simply not enough. I had, in the previous months, tried each line of reasoning, every avenue of "thinking" myself into a better frame of mind, and nothing had worked. Now I could clearly see why. Guilt could never be wiped away with thoughts! Only an act of God could do it!

The guilt of all the ages came crashing down around me that afternoon; I stood with the millions of lost sinners who had gone on before, and the verse "All have sinned and come short of the glory of God" broke like a splash of brilliant sunlight through dark gray clouds. I cried out from deep inside me, "My God, my God, *forgive me*. Me, Lord, me. Not my husband, not my children, not my successes or failures, not one single circumstance, just forgive me!"

I wept as I waited for forgiveness. My tears were not the bitter tears of an angered soul, but the tears of one truly penitent. As I waited, it slowly began to break into my consciousness that at the very first moment I had asked for forgiveness, God had instantly forgiven.

What joy, what incredible joy. The silent, yet expectant peace that followed in the next few moments was breathtaking. Nothing seemed to move, and I was suspended on the very wings of angels . . . rejoicing angels.

The cross of Christ appeared on the map spread out before me, and it completely replaced the scenes of my past. The empty tomb of Christ loomed eloquently on my map. It *was* empty! He was not there; He had risen and so would I. I would live because He is alive. It was the newest of new beginnings for me. I had just been born. I find it most difficult to describe this new birth except to say that I know the original, ugly Joyce Landorf had died, and emerging from her smoldering ashes was a totally new Joyce. Only the name was the same.

I could have laughed, sung, and danced with the great King David because I could finally identify with his words written so long ago when he said of God, "He would not have listened if I had not confessed my sins. But He listened! He heard my prayer! He paid attention to it! Blessed be God who didn't turn away when I was praying, and didn't refuse me His kindness and love" (Ps. 66:18-20).

The simplicity of that afternoon was truly unbelievable. The answer found in giving myself to Christ had been there all the time.

The filth and garbage of my sinful life began to pour out of me and from each hidden corner of my body and soul the stench began to lift and fade. Even now I can only explain those feelings in the barest of terms. It was like a morning at the beach when the haze and dense fog seem to hang there forever, but then as the noonday sun gets brighter, the haze vanishes, the depressing fog begins to move off, and the blue of the sky and sea are exactly as God intended: beautiful, clear, and shining. Gone is the morning gloom, and the loveliness of the day is overwhelming. So it was for me. What delirious joy!

The psalmist must have felt great guilt, for his joy at his forgiveness was obvious when he wrote:

> What happiness for those whose guilt has been forgiven! What joys when sins are covered over! What relief for those who have confessed their sins and God has cleared their record.
> There was a time when I wouldn't admit what a sinner I was. But my dishonesty made me miserable and filled my days with frustration.

All day and all night Your hand was heavy on me. My strength evaporated like water on a sunny day until I finally admitted all my sins to You and stopped trying to hide them. I said to myself, "I will confess them to the Lord." And You forgave me! All my guilt is gone! (Ps. 32:1-5).

Yes, yes, wise psalmist, I know! I *know!*

Looking back . . .

My life was spared that dreadful day by that call from a young minister named Chuck Leviton.

How many times in my life span had I met someone and responded, "Hello, it's nice to meet you," never dreaming the importance that casual meeting would have at some later time. That's just how I had met Chuck months before. Really it was sort of a fluke. Phil Kerr had asked me to fly to Phoenix, Arizona, for a Youth for Christ rally. I was in no condition to sing, physically, mentally, or spiritually, and I tried to beg off, but refusing Phil was not an easy thing to do, so . . . I went, stepped off the plane, and met Chuck Leviton. He was slight of build (he has now lost that in tribute to his wife's cooking), energetic, and outgoing in personality, and because of the way he used words, really communicating, I liked him immediately.

There were two other interesting facts about him: he was a go-getter and he was a converted Jew. Both facts set him a little apart from anyone else I had ever known.

I know now that his phone call was merely a desire to share those verses with me for whatever they might be worth. By the time I got around to telling him what actually had transpired that day, he had practically forgotten the call.

When I look back to the moment when I almost succeeded in taking my life, a thought repeatedly breathes out of me, *How could I? How could I have even thought such a thing?* In the past, whenever I had read of a millionaire or movie star committing suicide, I had always had the same chain of reactions: shock, sadness, and then the thought. *with their fame and money, I'd have figured out some other way!*

A wealthy socialite in Michigan took her life dressed in a $200 dressing gown in the bedroom of her nineteen-room Grosse Point house; even in those luxurious surroundings, she could find no reason to live. Can you imagine being in her position, with her fame and wealth, and not having a reason to live? It seems almost incredible, yet, while I never knew this woman personally, I am familiar with her reasoning, for I have dragged myself up the steps of those same rationalities, only to find the same tightly bolted door at the top.

"Money, fame, and success (usually in that order) will give us whatever it is we seek in life." That philosophy is mixed in with our pablum when we are babies, and we obediently swallow it until the moment of our disillusionment and then it sticks in our throats and gags us.

Why isn't money, fame, and success enough? And what's so bad about reaching out and grabbing everything we can while we can?

Perhaps it's because God made us in two parts, neatly put together, but two distinct pieces. One part is our body which we can see and touch; the other, our soul — untouchable, invisible, but undeniably there! We all take great pains to feed, clothe, bathe, and care for the physical body. We pamper it with vitamins and shots, take it to the dentist, and even in death we dress it in finery. So much for the body . . . what of the soul? It too was made for nourishment and care. When ignored, it begins to die of malnutrition. When it isn't bathed with God's forgiveness and cleansed of sin, it begins to die of filth and neglect. Sooner or later it presses the silent alarm button and pleads with the body, "Find me, feed me, clean me, and most of all, love me." If the body ignores the implorings of the soul, it soon loses its will to live. Skilled researchers who study the build-up to suicide are well aware that the act is preceded by deep depression. It's precisely at this point that the body and soul become so fatigued by depression that suicide seems the only logical way up and out. Here, too, is the moment when the millionaire or the famous movie star wakes up one morning with the frightening knowledge, "Half of me is dead (the inner half); why should the other half go on?" In the moments just before death they write a scribbled note which says in part, "There is nothing left inside. . . ."

I *now* know the amount of money and success you do or do not have hasn't the remotest connection with being happy, having peace of mind, or being alive to really live life.

When desperation rises to its crest, you identify with David, who centuries before had penned:

> My heart is in anguish within me. Stark fear overpowers me. Trembling and horror overwhelm me. Oh, for wings like a dove, to fly away and rest! I would fly to the far off deserts and stay there. I would flee to some refuge from all this storm (Ps. 55:4-8).

If I had read that in those moments, my heart would have cried out, "Me too, David, me too," and the razor would have easily found its mark. Thank God, He stopped me in time!

6

"O Lord my God, I pled with You, and You gave
me my health again.
You brought me back from the brink of the grave,
from death itself, and here I am alive!"

Psalm 30:2, 3

When I left that green wingbacked chair, I was still
wearing a pair of black Capris and a pink sweater, still married to Dick, still the mother of two children, and still living
in a messy house. Nothing about my surroundings had
changed, yet everything looked different. I knew I was
no longer the same person. It was getting late, and I suddenly realized I had the unique desire to cook a really
good dinner for Dick and my children. Now, this sounds
simple enough and not too earthshaking, but if you had im-
patiently burned or undercooked as many dinners as I had,
you would immediately grasp how spectacular this thought
was to me. I *really wanted* to cook dinner!

I fairly floated into my kitchen on wings of joy! I was a
newborn soul thrilled with the love of Christ, the forgiveness of Christ, and the presence of Christ. As I stood there
in the center of that room I thought, *Jesus Christ lives
within me. He is here right now . . . right here in my kit-*

chen. My dirty, filthy kitchen! The horror of those last four words filled me with the same sinking feeling you would have if twelve people in formals and tuxedos showed up for dinner and you were caught with your hair in pink rollers carrying out the garbage. I really saw my dirty kitchen (plus all the other rooms) for the first time, and I realized I could never in a million years ask the Lord of all beauty to share and live in such a filthy mess. I'm afraid that neglected kitchen never knew what hit it. No white tornado, just ninety-eight pounds of glorious new me, and aside from tackling the baked-on mess in the oven (a good two days of work), I had everything sparkling in a couple of hours.

In those two hours I had learned the most valuable lesson a housewife can ever learn. I had cleaned that kitchen, not because someone was coming over and I had to impress them, or because my husband had ordered it, but because God Himself would live, walk, and talk with me in the rooms of my house and I wanted everything to be in order.

I had washed the dishes, cleaned the sink, the counter tops, and the stove top, and using soap, bleach, water, and razor blades, managed to see the original color of the linoleum. And, amazingly, for the first time in my life, I did it *without resenting every single second.*

When I finished the last bit of scrubbing in the kitchen that day, I whispered, "There, Lord, doesn't that look beautiful? Thank you for this stove and sink, and honestly I'll try to cook something fit to eat tonight." Above every kitchen sink in the world should be written the instruction, "Whatsoever thy hand findeth to do, do it with thy might!"

It must have been around five o'clock when the first

awful doubt hit me. *This afternoon has been quite an experience for me. What if it was just some high-level emotional binge? What happens when Dick comes home? I cannot tell him about the razor blades. Has anything changed, really? When I see Dick, will it just be the same old nightmare?* Those ugly thoughts persisted.

One of our wedding presents had been a large mirror. I had placed it on a living room wall, and by standing directly in front of the kitchen stove I could clearly see the front door. That's where I was that night as Dick walked through the door. I thought for sure the mirror was kidding me. I was looking at the man I couldn't even stand to touch, the man I thoroughly resented, and the man I did not love; yet I had never seen him look so handsome, at least not for the last four years. He looked taller, more blond, and definitely "my type." Considering this was the same man I had begged and pleaded with the Lord to trade in on a newer model, you can see what a complete reversal of opinion this was. I casually rounded the corner of the kitchen table and met him halfway between the dining room and living room. He simply stood there, about three feet away, and said with quiet determination in his voice, "Joyce, I don't care what you think or say, but today I made up my mind. I am going to be a Christian. I mean, a real, honest-to-God Christian, a Christian husband and father." It was the most eloquent, dramatic grouping of words I had ever heard. He looked ten feet tall by then and was as handsome as a mythical Greek god.

Five years before we had been married, legally married, but in that one glorious moment, we were joined by God in holy matrimony. And while neither of us understood it all, we sensed that this day had brought about the beginning of a real, contemporary miracle.

It was after dinner before I found out about Dick's part of the miracle. (Incidentally, dinner was a smashing success, not counting the salad I forgot to get out of the refrigerator.) I knew I would not be able to share the events of my day for a long time, but I was eager to know what had so changed Dick.

He had gone to work that morning, resolved that somehow, someway this nightmare called marriage must dissolve. I had no idea that this cool, ice-water-in-the-veins man could be so emotionally distraught. He had already written a farewell letter and put it away with his things.

I have it before me now as I write this (we have kept it to reread occasionally to remind us of God's unbelievable love), and I can't look at it for even a moment without tears blurring my vision. It's a heartbreaking cry from the deepest depths of a man's soul and it ends with the words, "I see no hope; no hope at all for us, our marriage, our children, or for the future."

That afternoon Dick held the letter in his hand for a long time, and then across the envelope he slowly wrote, "To Joyce: when you find this I will be dead." Since the note would really be a last will and testament, he signed his name.

As nearly as he can recall, his thoughts ran like this: *Lord, I can't suffer like this any more; I am at the end of my rope. What are You trying to do to me? What do You want? You know there is no way out of this. What am I going to do?*

Then in the privacy of his small office, he heard these quiet, sure, steady words, "Dick, taking your life is not the answer; I want you. I want you to be the husband and father you should be. I've planned a life for you. I want you." The voice of stubborn love pleaded, and Dick felt himself irresistibly drawn to the Master. How could he resist such love? How could he turn away? How could anybody take his life and carry out a suicide threat once he had heard the hushed but clear tone of love in the Savior's voice?

He pushed the first button on his inter-office communications set and quietly told the girl at the other end he did not wish to be disturbed. Then, in an atmosphere of awesome reverence, he slipped out of his chair, knelt beside it, and he prayed the oldest prayer in the world, "Lord, forgive me."

It was about one o'clock in the afternoon. Way back in our youth group at church he had prayed prayers like this one, but this prayer was surrounded by a sense of delicate urgency. If this prayer was not answered and forgiveness did not come, then everything was all over. He had reached the end of himself. If God did not exist and did not hear, all was lost. "Lord, *really* come into my life. Make me the man *You* want me to be. I'm so tired of me, my goals, my demands. Make me the husband and father I should be. Now (he breathed his first breath of forgiven air), thank You. Thank You for the beginning."

We did have a long way to go, but it really was the day of beginning for us. We had survived major surgery; the cancerous sin had been cut out, and even though we had been at the threshold of death, we had pulled through. What was to follow would be a three-year recovery period; the incision and scar tissue would heal, but *very, very* slowly.

During our five years of marriage, sin had killed not only my innocence, but all creative ideas and productiveness as well. God would have to reawaken this part of me. Sin, in Dick, had killed off his goals. God would have to restore a new will, a new drive, and a fresh new way to love, work, and dream. We both knew the recovery would take time, and once more we were completely unprepared for God's patient, stubborn love.

Looking back . . .

I never started out to be a big sinner, liar, or colossal cheat. Things just seemed to move in that direction, much like a tiny snowball pushed down a hill. Slowly at first and then gathering momentum, it suddenly became huge and uncontrollable.

We never start out deliberately to break each of the Ten Commandments, but once we have turned our faces away from God's direction, it becomes easy to sin and, what's worse, to rationalize away our feelings of guilt.

One little sin inevitably leads to another; I shall not go into all the lurid details of my past except to say that in the first wretched five years of marriage I eventually broke every law.

"Even murder?" you ask.

"Oh, yes," I have to answer. Haven't you watched a critical tongue carve, tear, and shred up a human being?

Haven't you listened to an insidious piece of gossip and watched as two people suffocated in their marriage as a result. If you have, then you already know two of the devious ways of murdering someone.

"But what about adultery?" you ask. Yes, that too, but before you smugly gather your righteous skirts around you and say, "Well, thank goodness I've never committed *that* sin," remember it was Jesus who said, "Anyone who even looks at a woman with lust in his eye has already committed adultery with her in his heart" (Matt 5:28). A Christian man I know prides himself on the well-publicized fact that he has been true and faithful to his wife through all their married years, but when this same man looks at another woman, his lustful eyes make her feel stripped of her clothing and all decency. Is it adultery? You bet!

Then what about the woman who continually says to her husband, "If you made as much money as George," or "If you looked like Bob and dressed better," or "If you treated me like Stan treats his wife. . . . " All she is really saying is that she has spent a good deal of time looking at and, yes, lusting after someone else. According to our Lord, the sinful act has already been done.

I could identify with the woman caught in adultery and the incredible feelings she must have had after narrowly escaping being stoned to death. The words, "Go, and sin no more," must have rung in her heart like a sweet, forgotten melody. I knew all the sins I had committed, and I knew God was fully aware of them, too, but I also knew I had asked forgiveness and a full pardon had been given.

Along with forgiveness came a new lease on everyday living and practical Christianity.

It's always a surprising thing to me, even yet, that most of the important decisions are made in front of the stove or sink. Some highly original and thought-provoking questions are asked by our children on those hallowed spots, and often it is in front of the stove that I remind the Lord of His friend James who said, "If you want to know what God wants you to do, ask Him, and He will gladly tell you, for He is always ready to give a bountiful supply of wisdom to all who ask Him; He will not resent it" (James 1:5). Sometimes I've said that verse with tears of frustration streaming down my face; other times I've said it with the quiet desperate thought, *I am NEVER going to make it as a mother!* But so many times He has answered on the spot. If God doesn't work in the nitty-gritty of my kitchen, it doesn't make sense to serve Him!

Of course I had not only God's help in those early days, but Dick's as well. It has occurred to me that some readers may now be saying: "Why, after twenty-five years of praying, hasn't God converted my husband (or wife)?" I don't know why except that to God each individual is exquisitely different, and He deals with them accordingly. He knew just how desperate Dick and I were. The Bible reminds us that God will not tempt us beyond that we are able to bear, and only God seems to know how much we can take. I am reminded of so many situations in which, had you told me exactly what I would face in the following days, weeks, or months, I would have said, "Oh, no, I will not be able to stand it; I'll crack up." Yet, God knew precisely what my pressure points would bear and how His stubborn love would help me to endure unbelievable trials!

I remember the man in our church who accepted Christ after his wife had prayed for him for thirty-five years. With tears he told how he simply had to become a Christian because in thirty-five years he had not seen his wife do one unkind, unloving, or unchristian thing. I wept too, for I was never that kind of wife in those days before learning about God's loving habits.

7

"He has given me a new song to sing, of praises
to our God. Now many will hear of the glorious
things He did for me, and stand in awe before the
Lord, and put their trust in Him."   Psalm 40:3

I've given much thought to those early years of discovery
and recovery, and I find it strange, yet true, that immediately after our decision to become Christians, Dick and I
faced the greatest disappointments and setbacks in our lives.
One involved my singing.

For the first time since I had started singing seriously at
thirteen, I had a song to sing. All along I had vocal chords,
the ability to sing and carry a tune, but the lyrics were sadly
missing.

Now, songs, glorious songs, were welling up from my
heart and I wanted to sing them from the rooftops; however,
Chuck Leviton, by now a precious friend in Christ, suggested that I record them instead.

Before you could say "recording," I was walking into
Radio Recorders Studio, facing an entire orchestra, and recording an album!

The recording session was a total disaster! I was so incredibly bad and many problems developed.

The album was sold to an eastern recording company and I was off on a 3,000 mile tour as soloist for the Bob Shepard Chorale to publicize the release of my album. I didn't want to go, as I knew how long I would be away. (We gave twenty-one concerts in twenty-three days.) After all, I had just found the Lord and what I had been missing as a wife and mother all those years, and to leave it all was unthinkable. Both my husband and parents talked me into it, however, and sent me on my way.

The first stop was nonscheduled in the middle of a California desert as the bus (named "Flattery" because it got us nowhere) had its first of three hundred flat tires. I should have wired Dick and called the entire thing off right then, but God had quite a lesson to teach me, so I stayed with it.

The record company was to send the new album ahead and meet us in Phoenix for a Youth for Christ rally, but the album did not arrive in time . . . it did not arrive at all. Here we all were — publicizing an album which was not available. Finally, on the main platform at Winona Lake at the National Convention of Youth for Christ, I faced the president of the company with one question: "Where *is* the album?"

With complete sophistication he calmly answered, "We don't like the album so we are not going to release it."

I recovered momentarily to question, "You mean you are going to throw a $5,000 album away — just like that?"

"No," he answered, "we are simply going to take your

voice off the voice track, dub someone else's voice on it, and release it next week." *Which he did!!*

I stumbled off the platform and, in the midst of that great convention with thousands of people around, tried to find someone I knew. Dick had joined me for the last few days of the tour, but I couldn't find him anywhere. Besides, when you're really crying hard, your vision is less than perfect. I did manage to find our car and crawled in — the pain was suffocating me.

This part of the recovery I did not understand. Wasn't I God's child now? Didn't I have a song to sing? Wasn't it miraculous the way the Lord had opened the doors for this album? Why had I come all those tiring miles, leaving my children and home, to be brutally crushed by this blow? Why was all this happening?

The only thing I heard from the still, small voice was, "Trust Me."

"But Lord," I wept, "I have, I am, and I will, but look what's happened."

I dried my tears (not then, but three days later) and went home after finishing my commitment with the tour. I began to realize I had done too much too soon after surgery. I had a lot of healing yet to take place, and the Lord had many lessons left before I was to go out into the world to share my good news. As I look back on it now, it seems that some of those lessons were similar to the ones Moses learned in the wilderness — especially the ones about "waiting on the Lord" and "being still."

Not too long after I returned home from that disastrous tour, I shared my doubts and feelings with my mother. Why was God doing this? Hadn't I been through enough hell?

What else did God want? How could I ever know what He really wanted? Why had He given me this opportunity to sing and then put me through such torture? Was He trying me and testing me because of my past sins? If He was, would I ever be really free from those sins?

Mother was quiet as she studied me from across the table and then thoughtfully said, "No, this time of testing has nothing to do with past sins. Those sins are under the blood of Christ, and either God can forgive sins or He lied. Furthermore," she went on, "if He did not lie and has forgiven you, then you must be willing to forgive yourself or you will *make* God into a liar."

Then sensing the real problem, she did a lovely thing. She leaned across the kitchen table, cupped her hands around my face, and prayed, "Lord, dear Lord, heal Joyce's memories; heal the bitter memories, the sad memories, and all the angry memories."

That simple to-the-heart-of-the-matter prayer flowed over me like fragrant oil, soothing as it reached every part of me. It was the first time I could think of those past sins and *know* forgiveness, and it was suddenly very clear that as I thought of the recording company in the East, my heart was at a peaceful rest. The freedom of that moment was intoxicating, and my recovery was showing great progress.

I decided that someday, maybe, I would make an album, but it would be in God's time, if it was to be at all. Meanwhile, I would go out and sing for God's glory with my new song. But a funny thing happened to me on my way to sing . . . no one asked me! Not one single person asked me to sing! Not even my biased-about-my-singing parents.

No one called, wrote, or even hinted that they would like to have me sing for them.

Several times a day I checked it out, rather casually at first, with the Lord, "Lord, You *did* give me this voice, didn't You? Don't You want me to serve You?" Then I spied, all fresh and new, the verse about the harvest being ready and laborers so few, and in genuine seriousness I began to petition the Lord to use me. Still no one asked! I couldn't ring somebody up on the phone and tell them I was available. (I did try that several times, and it had such a devastating effect on those people that they still don't speak to me, much less ask me to sing!)

One morning, as I prayed about this whole business of singing, God proposed a shocking question: "Would you be willing *never* to sing in public again?" Thinking I had misunderstood the question, I rephrased it for Him, "You mean, would I be willing *to sing* in public again?"

"No," came the firm answer. "I asked, would you be willing to stop singing in public?"

It took two full weeks for the magnitude of that question to really reach me, and after those fourteen, agonizing prayer-spent days, I finally had an answer. I had weighed carefully my past life and knew I never wanted to go back to that routine, but I also was aware of the marvelous song exploding in my heart and on my lips continually, so I said, "All right, Lord, how does this sound? I won't ever sing in public again. . . ." (I had committed myself to doing what God would ask, to walking the road He would choose, and even though I did not understand such a request, I would be His obedient girl.) "But, Lord, since I have no idea what to do about this beautiful song inside me, do You mind if I sing, just for You, every day for the rest of my life?" His approving answer began one of the most magnificent changes in my life.

The next morning I gave a concert in my dark, empty living room — a concert just for my unseen Lord. His presence grew very precious, and the songs in front of me took on new life. The quality of my singing expanded, breath control seemed less of a problem, and phrasing became second nature to me. HE was teaching me to sing, and at the end of that first session I didn't care if I ever sang for any audience. What I had in my own living room, before my own piano, was the most thrilling experience I had ever known.

I found God was not particularly interested in my surrendering my voice or talent, but more directly, He found the place of my resistance; and where I was resisting Him the most was the very portal through which He wanted to work. It's easy to give Him what we are eager to surrender, but at what point do we resist Him? He'll find it and that's exactly what He'll demand from us.

The procedure of singing every day, alone with Him, has never stopped; unless I am ill, time is spent each day in this unique way of praising God.

The first month went by with no one asking me to sing . . . the second . . . and finally the sixth. What amazed me was that it was perfectly all right with me. I had accepted the position of singing a private concert for my Lord each day, and if that was all He wanted me to do, I was at ease. (I have the same peace about writing articles and books. God asked me to write. He did not tell me to publish any of it — just write. My collection of rejection letters from publishers is in a folder marked, "Remember, He said write — not publish!") Those days became the first since I had started singing that were free from worry or frustrations about a "career." Wonder of wonders, too, I had been freed from my jealousy of other singers, especially those with albums. And to this day, being on a program with another soprano doesn't do anything negative at all, but is usually enjoyable. Perhaps only singers reading this will understand exactly what I mean, but only God could have worked that kind of miracle.

One day after six months of private concerts, God woke me up early and said, "You are ready now to sing for Me in public performances." I responded, "Who, me?"

I had to go to Reseda to visit my mother that same day, and I don't think I'd been in the house five minutes when she asked me to sing. For the second time in one day I said, "Who, me?" She sat across the room on a curved sofa as I began to play the piano and sing. I saw her straighten up, lean forward, and listen as if she was hearing me for the first time. When I finished and looked directly at her, she was sitting erect and her deep brown eyes were blazing intently upon me. All she said was, "What's happened to you?"

"Why, mother?" I asked.

"You sound so different, so full of direction; the anxiousness has left your voice."

I was unable to tell her everything about the events of those past six months, but I did share bits and pieces with her. I told her of the presence of God in my life and about the amazing Holy Spirit who was as real as breathing. Then I told her about singing for the Lord each day and shared what I was learning about the Composer of all music and the changes that were taking place.

After mother's death two years ago, I found in her diary her thoughts about that day's conversation:

> Joyce, to you,
> Your experience of Monday, the eleventh, was a divine fragrance, a sweetness, an overflowing joy, and pure love imparted to your soul by the Spirit of God. He has invaded you and a sacred union has permeated your entire being. This is not a single, fleeting experience, but it is yours as you hold communion with God. He will come for every needed task for *His* glory and *your* joy. "Not by might, nor by power (human effort and energy), but by MY spirit." What once had been painful trying now becomes perfect trusting. Weakness has been turned into strength, sighing into joyful song, and human failure into triumph . . . all because of Him.

Mother had never failed to hold me up before the throne of God many times a day, and many more times during the night. I had too brief a span of time to tell her how I loved her, but when she did leave us for heaven, she knew of my love, and I had communicated my gratefulness for the steadfastness of her prayer life.

I don't know how so many people learned I was available to accept singing engagements, but in a mysterious way, God touched the hearts of many people; my phone began to ring with requests, and I stepped out to sing. Without asking to sing, without running any ads or promotion, and without any exposure, I was singing!

Some two years later the Lord tapped me on the shoulder and said, "Now is the time to make another recording." The album "Peace Through the Lord" was born.

Once I had the album completed, the first song I set the

needle on was "A Heart That's Touched by Thee," and I wept. The surgery had been nothing less than perfect. Even as I heard the song playing, I thought of two words, "Trust Me," and I repeated, "I *have*, I *am* and I *will*."

> A heart that's touched by Thee, Oh God,
> Lord make it so today,
> A heart that's touched by Thee, Oh God,
> What more is there to say?
>
> I'll give you all my talents, Lord,
> Yes, all to you I bring,
> And promise now from this day forth
> Only of You will I sing.
>
> If You will touch my heart, Oh Lord,
> And purify within,
> And purge out all the self and pride,
> Cleanse me from all my sin.
>
> I long to sing thy wondrous praise,
> To walk and talk for Thee.
> So give me now, Oh Lord, I pray,
> A heart that's touched by thee.[1]

The sweetest singer of all time was the psalmist David, and I think his secret formula for singing is found in his writings.

"But as for me, I will sing each morning about Your power and mercy. For You have been my high tower of refuge, a place of safety in the day of my distress.

"O my Strength, to You I sing my praises; for You are my high tower of safety, my God of mercy" (Ps. 59:16, 17).

If my singing reaches out, touches, warms, and maybe breaks down some barriers in my audiences, it is only be-

---

[1] "A Heart That's Touched by Thee," © 1958 by Joyce Landorf. Words by Chuck Leviton. Music by Joyce Landorf.

cause of Him. I can't think of a single reason why He should use me, yet He does! And if this chapter on singing has a moral, it is this: Don't ask to be used. Ask Him to make you usable. It takes longer that way, but the harvest is greater.

Looking back . . .

Too often we are so eager to share this wonderful, new, exciting venture called faith; we race ahead of God's plan. A man quits his insurance job and feels he should go into the ministry. A woman feels led to start a Bible class and stops being a wife. Both feelings flow naturally from this new-found joy bubbling inside of them, and I do not mean to imply that they should not tell the world about it. But I am saying there must be a period of growing and learning before we pull up our roots and go running all over the country giving our testimony to packed houses.

We are like the movie star I know who accepted Christ and a few weeks later was speaking before huge crowds. Many of the people in her audiences were completely disillusioned some months later when she fell off the platform dead drunk. What happened? Did she have an experience with God or not? Yes, but in a few weeks the wounds of sin had no time to heal. She couldn't see what God wanted from her, nor did she have time to grow in the Word of God, so she suffered a major setback. In the case of this movie star, the result was devastating to her testimony.

Coming to Christ is similar to a complicated surgery. Christ, as the great physician and surgeon, cuts out the cancerous sin of our old life, sutures the incision, and sends us off to the recovery room and intensive care. To stagger out of that recovery room, hold a press conference and tell everybody what a marvelous doctor we've had and what miraculous surgery has been completed would be nothing short of suicide.

"Be still and wait."

8

"For I cried to Him and He answered me! He freed me from all my fears.
Others too were radiant at what He did for them. Theirs was no downcast look of rejection!"

Psalm 34:4, 5

How does God begin a healing, restoring work in a marriage that is not just sick, but dead? We knew one thing; this part of our recovery was going to have its setbacks too, so we cautiously began the daily business of living together . . . which brings us right back to the toothpaste tube. (Would you believe we changed to powder?)

The first thing that seemed to take place was simply talking to one another. Remember how you talked for hours and hours when you were dating? I used to talk with Dick three hours on a date, come home, phone him, and talk another two hours.

However, talking to each other had, in five years of marriage, become a lost art. We had to learn not only how to speak, but more important, how to listen. It wasn't easy.

When the communication lines were open to the Lord, it seemed to tune us into an entire world of words. We began to talk about the goals each of us thought we should have in our marriage, and to my surprise I found that Dick's goal was "X" amount of dollars per year. My goal was a five-bedroom house. As we talked about those aims, we realized, while they weren't necessarily wrong, they seemed shallow and inadequate. Even if we achieved them, would they really bring about the kind of marriage we wanted? We highly doubted it, so we began to formulate some meaningful objectives for our new life together.

Naturally, we talked of the irritating personality traits in each other. To my surprise, when I told Dick some of the things he was doing that really bothered me, he hadn't dreamed I was upset about them. He is a "conscientious door-closer," and I rarely cooked a meal without his following me around in the kitchen slamming doors or drawers. I'd reach for a knife from the silver drawer, cut something at the stove, swing back to get the slotted spoon, and crack my hand smack into the closed drawer. When I told him how much this bothered me, he said sincerely, "I was only trying to be helpful."

All this talk finally led to the business of my messiness and his neatness. We both had plenty to say, but I began to notice for the first time in our marriage that I had a real desire to be neater. Being completely neat will never be my cup of tea, but at this point I began to be a little neater and Dick to be a little messier. (Not really, but if things were not in their ABSOLUTELY right order, he could overlook it.) It was the first step in total loving. As long as we live and love together, we will always have these human traits, and total loving helps you to accept all the good ones and, yes, even the bad. When I began adding up all the traits in Dick that were admirable, I could see the list was quite long, but his neatness and his stubbornness were a part of his personality too, so I would accept them as well. I had married him for better or for worse. When I accepted this, I found a deep peace, and my first act was to hang all the toilet tissue rolls in the right direction (Dick's way). And what surprised me the most was that I felt no resentment; in fact, I couldn't change things fast enough.

When Dick told me about my reckless spending of money, I realized that often I had impulsively bought something just to spite him. I remember for years I begged, nagged, and haggled about his buying me a mink-trimmed sweater. It was while we were in this early talk stage and walking through a department store that I spotted the mink-trimmed sweaters fifteen tables ahead of us. I knew we would soon pass them, but as we neared the counter, the knowledge that I did not *have* to have *anything* swept over me. I looked up at Dick and thought, "Whatever it was I felt I needed before, I surely don't need now . . . not with Dick by my side."

I intended to walk right past the sweater counter, but just as we got there, guess who said, "Hey, wait; I want to see these." That's right, the very same husband who would not even look at the newspaper advertisements about these sweaters and who for years had glared at me when I talked about them! He was going through the sweaters like a little old lady at a rummage sale. When he found the right one, he held it up to me.

"Oh, honestly, Dick," I said. "Let's go; you know I don't need this, and besides, we can't begin to afford it."

"I know," he answered, "but I want you to know that if

we had the money, this is the one I'd buy you because you'd look just stunning in it!"

I thought of all those wasted years of nagging, and I asked the Lord, right there on the second floor of that department store, to give me many years to smother that wonderful husband of mine with love and kindness. I also resolved to curb my wild desire to buy, buy, buy, so someday I could be trusted with our checkbook. (So far I'm doing all right, with only an occasional slip-up on those after-Christmas sales each year.)

What a gigantic relief it was to be able to open up, talk, and discuss all these things. It was only natural that the second thing that took place was our getting into the Word of God. At first it was separately, then together, and now it's both. It was incredible that anyone could have heard the Scriptures backwards and forwards and then go back over the same ones again and find them brand new, yet that's exactly how they were — brand new. We knew they were the same verses we had heard in church, but the entire Book of Ephesians seemed to have been written for us. "Was *that always* there?" I found myself asking time and time again.

I remember the day I found John 10:10. I phoned Dick, "Listen to this, just listen to this," I screamed joyfully.

"Joyce, I'm trying to," he answered patiently.

"This is for us . . . this is all ours! It says, 'I am come that you might have life and have it more abundantly.'"

For two people who had had so little life they were willing to throw what they did have away, here was the most exciting promise we had ever read.

"Oh, honey, to think we almost missed this life — to think

we came so close to never knowing God's abundant plan for us and now to read these words of Christ and to know He's talking to us . . . I can't believe it, yet I know it's true!" John 10:10 became our verse. David must have had a similar experience because he wrote, "But as for me, I came so close to the edge of the cliff! My feet were slipping and I was almost gone" (Ps. 73:2). He almost slipped off too!

I was stunned again a few days later when I read Romans 6:11. This time I called my mother. "Mother, did you know that Romans 6:11 is a long verse?" All my life I had thought it had only five words in it, "Reckon yourselves dead unto sin." I had heard so many legalistically pointed sermons on that verse that I found it utterly amazing to discover the verse continued, "but *alive* unto God." For twenty-five years I had thought it ended in the middle. What a discovery! So many sermons on being dead, dead, dead, and not enough on being alive, alive, alive!

As we really began devouring the Bible, we were both struck by the word "forgiveness." Especially the forgiveness in the fourth chapter of Ephesians. Can you image how we felt when we read these words, having just come out of five angry, terrible years of arguments and fighting?

> And do not grieve the Holy Spirit of God, (do not offend, or vex, or sadden Him) by Whom you were sealed (marked, branded as God's own, secured) for the day of redemption — of final deliverance through Christ from evil and the consequences of sin.
> Let all bitterness and indignation *and* wrath (passion, rage, bad temper) and resentment (anger, animosity) and quarreling (brawling, clamor, contention) and slander (evilspeaking, abusive or blasphemous language) be banished from you, with all malice (spite, ill will or baseness of any kind).

> And become useful *and* helpful *and* kind to one another, tenderhearted (compassionate, understanding, loving-hearted), forgiving one another [readily and freely], as God in Christ forgave you (Eph. 4:30-32, Amplified New Testament).

Dick and I had tried on so many occasions during our five years to intelligently reason the problems out, and we only ended by generating more frustration and bitterness.

As I reread those last lines in Ephesians, I wondered how I could have *ever* forgiven Dick until God had forgiven me. After experiencing God's forgiveness and remembering how instant and loving it was, this was the basis that enabled me to forgive Dick and all the other people in my life.

I found I had to forgive Dick for a lot of things, including his being so smart. His mathematical knowledge has enabled him to be a fine banker. His coolness and even temperament have been an outstanding asset in every position he's held, and his ability to work conscientiously has promoted him to the top position in every job. It seems strange to say you have to forgive someone for these "good" things, but I realized that I had been resentful of all these attributes. Now as I began to forgive him, I was finding a new freedom. It was that rare kind of freedom that only comes when we have experienced real forgiveness ourselves. What was resentment turned to a deep sense of pride. My attitudes did an about-face.

Dick, on the other hand, had to forgive me for my talents. He had deeply resented all the rehearsals, choirs, fellow singers, and musicians; just let a little old lady ask him how it felt to be married to such a "beautiful singer" and he'd come close to smashing her into the nearest woodwork. Whenever I sang, he would take his usual bored stance and wait the thing out. His face said, "Oh, when will all this be over so I can go home?" When I accused him of being jealous of my music, he simply said I was being ridiculous. Yet, if I was late from a choir rehearsal, I would find him waiting in near hysteria and blind rage.

About a year after we really became Christians, I was asked to sing in a large church. As I began my solo, I saw Dick, way in the back of the church as usual, but he was staring at me intently and was sitting on the extreme edge of his chair. When the service was over, he ran down that long aisle, picked me up by my arms and shoulders, held me high in the air, and said, "You have the most beautiful voice in the whole world!" It was as if he'd never, ever heard me sing in all of his life, but when God opened his ears he heard the Lord's joyous song. By God's forgiveness through Christ, Dick had the ability and freedom to forgive me, and his resentments toward my musical talents turned into pride. I know today when someone asks him how it feels to be married to such a "wonderful singer," his enthusiastic answer is, "Fascinating!"

As our Bible reading progressed, I continually had the same experience; it *always* fell open to the part about the husband being the head of the home or the part about wives submitting to husbands. For a few months I simply ignored the entire business, but I realized that even when I wasn't watching the Bible fall open to that place, I was thinking about it, and it was beginning to really bug me.

I knew that behind every successful man in America there was a woman pushing, pulling, and tugging at all the strings. The old Biblical idea of a man being the head of the home had always been *too* much for sophisticated, modern, outspoken me, and I didn't buy it!

I would love my husband's faults, forgive him, and shower him with understanding, but it would be a fifty-fifty deal.

But a real marriage is never a fifty-fifty deal. I've noticed that the couples who try it are continually counting up the score to see whose turn it is to give in and sometimes I've even heard them argue about whose turn it was the last time.

No, it seemed to me the fifty-fifty idea would have to go. Wherever two people worked or played or lived, somebody was always the pacesetter, the boss, the go-aheader, the president, the teacher, the dean, etc. *One* has *got* to be the leader!

I was never so aware of this principle until one day when I was shopping with my mother. Because of Christ's love I had found a new love for my family, and I had determined in my heart to show them more than enough love in whatever years were left . . . which brings us to the front door of a department store.

I held the door open and said, "After you, mother."

She said, "Oh, no, dear, you go ahead."

I laughed and said, "No, no, no; age before beauty you know."

"Now please, honey," she said, "I love you and you're my daughter; you go first."

"No, mother, I respect and honor you, so — YOU go first."

That skirmish ended in a draw because an elderly gentleman, weary of waiting, opened both doors and we walked through together. Then we saw the candy counter.

Mother dearly loved coconut and chocolate, so I stopped to get some, and we had quite a conversation about who was going to pay; we had the same conversation at the slipper counter and at the sale table on bath towels. By the time we had finished shopping and were back at the front door, I was in no mood to play out this little vignette again, so I said, "Mother, wherever two people exist, live, and play together, one of them must take the lead. One of them must make the final decisions. One of them must be boss. You and I are going to settle this thing right now, for the last time." So, it was there on a little settee by the department store door that my mother agreed; I was to open the doors, but she was to walk through first. She would be the boss as to where we went and how long we stayed. I don't believe you could say either one of us "gave up" anything; on the contrary, we both gained a great deal from it, and it certainly made shopping a lot easier.

This all made sense to me — letting one be the leader, but "head" of the home? I didn't quite know.

I began to pray at great length about who would lead in our marriage, and each time it was as if the Lord said, "You're making too much out of all this; just do as I say, trust Me, and you'll see My way is right." Well, you don't just rush into making your husband boss — what if he picks up the nearest whip and chair and snarls, "Ah, ha! This is precisely what I have been waiting for." But the quiet voice was there and stubbornly persisting, sooooo . . .

I decided that if I could trust God's word about forgiveness, then possibly I could trust Him on submission and head-of-the-house stuff. I wasn't too sure, but I'd give it a try.

That night I said, rather haltingly, "Dick, I hate to tell you this, but I am going to make you the president of the

Landorf Corporation." I said this with I-know-I'll-be-sorry-tomorrow written all over my face. But — guess who he made vice-president? That's right — ME! It was quite a surprise, and I was totally unprepared for it. How often we pray, just *sure* the worst thing will happen; and instead, a better, more glorious answer is given, and we feel like such monumental fools. How was I to know Dick was reading the same chapters? There is a lovely Scripture that reminds us: *before* we call He answers us.

Over and over Dick had read and thought about "loving your wife as your own self." It was dawning on him, brightly and clearly, that the first step to truly loving your wife was to love yourself. How to love oneself is another thing! Looking into the mirror one day he saw the face of a man who had been bought with a price; a man who had experienced a miracle; a man who, on some days, was not completely proud, but nevertheless a man who showed promise; a man . . . a new man . . . because of Christ. *He liked that man.* The rest was easy.

Our marriage definitely has the president and vice-president arrangement, and if this works so well in my husband's bank and in thousands of companies all over the world, think how well it works with both parties as one before the Lord.

The Landorf Corporation president never plans or executes moves without checking with his vice-president. On the other hand, this vice-president doesn't make decisions without checking with her president. There are meetings between us, and often the advice of the vice-president is taken and used, but it is the president who makes the final decision. Often the president will say to his vice-president,

"You have more knowledge on this subject, so you make the complete decision." This doesn't detract from his position; quite the contrary, it makes him an even greater man. But HE has the last word.

Time and time again, the president has said to this vice-president, "Hon, I don't think it should be done that way, but I'd like to get your thinking on it." Who could resist when it's put that way? So, then I tell him why I've proceeded in such a manner. Sometimes it's been left that way; other times he changes my thinking; and sometimes, because of God's wisdom, we come up with a third solution.

When I asked the Lord what He wanted for me and my new life, it seemed to be three things:

1. A wife to Dick
2. A mother to our children
3. A singer, writer, decorator, choir member, PTA member, etc.

Being a wife to Dick consumes energy, time, talent, and every ounce of intelligence I have and I wouldn't have it any other way. I've asked God to make me the perfect wife, knowing full well on some days I'll never make it, but I aim in that direction.

Dick came through our doorway the other night, and after he had kissed me he said, very tenderly, "I really love you."

I asked, "How come?"

A big grin spread all over his face; he shook his head and said, "Because you're always in there trying."

Another thing that helps our marriage is that we *like* each other. I really, truly like my husband. I like him as a husband, as a father to our children, as a dear friend, and even as a businessman. Before love comes like. Some of us reverse the order and wonder where the romance has gone.

Not too long ago I spoke and sang for a mother and daughter banquet at the First Baptist Church of Las Vegas, and on the short flight home the man seated next to me said,

"Been on a little holiday?"

"No," I answered, "I've been working."

His eyes widened, then brightened as he asked, "What kind of work do you do in Vegas?"

"I'm a singer," I said straight-faced.

His interest really came alive as he leaned over a bit and asked, "Were you on the stage?"

"Well," I paused, "as a matter of fact, I was."

"Really? Where?"

"You'll never believe it," I said and I told him.

His facial expression ran from ardent interest to the incredible you've-got-to-be-kidding. For some time he sat there just sizing me up, but when the stewardess came by, he asked me if he could buy me a drink. By the time I'd turned down a drink and a cigarette, he knew he was sitting by a very weird lady. He settled back in his seat to study me, and since I knew approximately what he was thinking, I said to him, "You're right; I don't drink; I don't smoke; I sing in churches. But if you think that's rare, I can go you one better . . . I'm happily married."

"Oh, well, little lady," he puffed, "I've been married twenty-five years, and I'm happily married."

"I think I'm more happily married than you," I countered, "and furthermore, I can ask you two questions that will prove it."

"Go ahead," he shot back.

"Okay, do you love your wife?"

"Man, yes, I love her," he boomed out good and loud. "This year I bought her a mink coat she's always yapped about; I let the decorators make a fortune on our apartment; and for Christmas I gave her a diamond that would knock your eyes out. Yes, ma'am, I love her!" (Now isn't that quaint! I asked him if he loved her, and he gave me a financial report.)

"Now, here's my second question," I said. "Do you like her?"

He blinked and shifted uneasily in his seat, and I wondered if he would answer honestly. I didn't wonder long because he said quite quietly, "No, I don't like her at all. That's why I'm on the road so many months out of the year." He continued, "You've won. You're right. You probably are more happily married — a lot more."

Until the plane touched down at Los Angeles International Airport, I told him about the kind of marriage Christ could give him, about liking someone because you are finally able to like yourself, and about the miraculous compatibility you can find in marriage because of God's love. I haven't seen him since, and I'll probably never see him again, but I have prayed and thought of him many times.

That night as I drove home from the airport, I relived a few scenes in my life that showed me how much Dick likes me. For instance, in all these years of marriage, Dick knows I've never cleaned out the refrigerator. (We don't have a dirty one because HE cleans it.) He came into our bedroom the other night with a Tupperware ® dish in his hands and said, "Now that it's got green growing on the top, can we throw it away?"

What warmed my heart was his understanding smile as he left the room. He likes me even though he knows me. He has accepted all of me — good points and bad points.

On the other hand, I like him even though I know we are going to have the same ridiculous conversation each night of our lives. He says, "Joyce, did you lock the back door?"

I answer, "Yes, Dick, I locked the back door."

His asking doesn't bother me, but his getting up and *checking* could send me up the wall screaming — except that his checking is part of his personality and I am committed to liking and loving the whole man.

The Scripture that tells us about the prayer, "Create in me a clean heart, O God; and renew a right spirit within me" (Ps. 51:10, KJV) was made for just this kind of daily living. Because God renews a right spirit (attitude) in us, we are able to *like* our mate and vice-versa.

God did so much in those early days to reconstruct our attitudes, and He continues to do so. The growing process never seems to stop.

Making Dick the head of our home was the first step in building our home. He became the head in little matters as well as the serious ones. For instance, I stopped serving asparagus (I love it and Dick absolutely loathes it) and I began serving eggplant (Dick loves it and I've finally learned how to gussie it up and make it taste all right to me). With each morning came an awareness that to succeed as God's new creature I would have to concentrate on being the wife I'd never been. So with the new day ahead of me, I read and reread Ephesians 4:22-24:

> Strip yourselves of your former nature — put off and dis-
> card your old unrenewed self — which characterized your
> previous manner of life and becomes corrupt through lusts
> *and* desires that spring from delusion;
>
> And be constantly renewed in the spirit of your mind —
> having a fresh mental and spiritual attitude;
>
> And put on the new nature (the regenerate self) created
> in God's image, (Godlike) in true righteousness and holi-
> ness (Amplified New Testament).

It was a rare and lovely thing when I realized since Jesus had left this earth He had sent back, to take His place with us, the Holy Spirit . . . and it would be the presence of the Holy Spirit that would guide me into that daily renewal of God's image. I did not have to try to be good, I simply had to allow the Holy Spirit freedom within my intellect, will, and emotions. He would do the rest.

Looking back . . .

Everywhere I turn these days I find people discussing their inability to communicate. Some people talk, but nobody understands their language; others talk, but never complete a thought; still others are just now learning that mere words are not enough to communicate.

Actually, talking has been an "in" thing for some time now. I was rereading the Genesis story of Adam and Eve, and with somewhat of a jolt I realized they were created for one lovely purpose. Do you remember what that was? *To talk with God!* Their whole day was spent in anticipation of the moment when, in the cool of the evening, God Him-self would come down and talk with them. As long as they were in the right relationship with Him, the channels of communication were wide-open. It was only after their sin-ning that the first silent, cold war was started. We can hear the warm, loving voice of God calling through the beautiful but empty garden, "Adam, where art thou?" and the chilling silence is terribly familiar.

It is my own personal belief that when men and women are not talking to God in a clear, vertical channel, the horizontal channel to their husband, wife, relatives, neighbors, and friends becomes hopelessly clogged. At least that's the way it was with us. But talking is only part of communicating.

I am in radio broadcasting and have had my own daily program for over five years now, so I should know something about communicating, but I find I'm still learning. I suppose it's because we communicate in a great many ways other than verbally. I have been told that we only communicate seven percent verbally. Thirty-eight percent is in the tone and pitch of our voice, and fifty-five percent in our facial expression. If we are able to express our trust and love in all these non-verbal areas, as well as with words, we are able to truly communicate. Once we learn how to be totally honest in pouring out our hearts to God, it never again is quite so difficult to speak, feel, and understand our families, neighbors, or friends. I say total honesty because when I tell my children, "I am a Christian," they are measuring my statement by what I'm like on Monday morning when it's raining, I haven't finished making their lunches, and they are going to be late for school — again. My statement of dedication means little to them if it's not backed up by honest living.

Really communicating with my husband opened up my eyes to all the facets of his personality. New talents developed in him that I never knew existed; his sense of humor must have always been there, but suddenly it began to emerge, and more than once I wondered who was writing his material. In fact, how like God to take the very things we hated about each other and turn them about-face so we could love them. Dick's German stubbornness was changed into strength. It is one of the qualities of Dick's personality that I now love the most.

> God give us men! A time like this demands
> Strong minds, great hearts, true faith and ready hands;
> Men whom the lust of office does not kill;
> Men whom the spoils of office cannot buy;
> Men who possess opinions and a will;
> Men who have honor, — men who will not lie!
>
> — *Josiah Gilbert Holland*

All this had come about because of one afternoon in a green wingbacked chair.

Do you remember the story of the father who was minding his little son for the afternoon but was still trying to get some studying done? His son simply would not leave him alone, and in fatherly desperation, he hit on a plan to keep the little boy occupied for at least an hour. He saw a map of the world and explained to his son that this was a picture of our hemisphere. He also said that he was going to tear the picture into pieces, and if the boy would put them back together, he would be rewarded with a surprise. The father then left the room confident that he would not be disturbed for the rest of the afternoon. Imagine his surprise when the son soon called him to the other room to see the finished puzzle. Sure enough, there on the carpet was the map.

"How did you do this?" the astonished father asked. "You don't know what the world looks like."

9

"You are my hiding place from every storm of life;
You even keep me from getting into trouble! You
surround me with songs of victory."   Psalm 32:7

When the children were just babies, being a mother was
a wonderful new adventure. Dressing up Rick and Laurie
and taking them out was pure delight, because everywhere
we went people commented on our beautiful children. Rick's
enormous sky-blue eyes and dark lashes could stop traffic,
and Laurie's pixie face and outrageously friendly personality
kept us in a constant stream of conversation with people in
stores, on the street, and in restaurants, providing us with
endless hours of entertainment. However, as Dick and I began to sink deeper into marital problems, serious things began happening in our roles as parents. I've already told you
about all the accidents we experienced, but how much men-
tal damage I did to both the children will never be known.
I can only ask God to forgive me and pray the damage was
not permanent.

My temper was terrible. I can vividly recall threatening
my children fifty times a day with sentences like, "If you
don't pick up those toys, I'm going to lose my temper and

then you'll be sorry." Many a spanking was given to them in a blind, all-consuming rage. I demanded obedience from them with an iron fist. They would do things right, or I'd make them. If I didn't lose my temper, certainly I never found my patience. I wanted things done and done yesterday.

After we became Christians, my attitude about being a mother made a complete about-face, and my temper and lack of patience took a turn for the better. But every once in awhile these two former-self enemies would raise their ugly heads and spit their awful venom. It always bothered me, because in the midst of those hysterical outbursts I could hear, in the distant past, a man yelling, "All right, you blasted kids, sit down and shut up . . . we're gonna read from the Bible," and the comparison was quite disturbing.

When the children were eight and ten, I was asked to travel as a soloist for Biola College. It was on the third week of that tour, way up in Bellingham, Washington, that I ran headlong into Dr. Henry Brandt. You don't crash into Henry and ever come out the same — he's such a big man in stature, mind, and heart.

The staff members for the conference ate all their meals together, and it took me almost the full week, three meals a day, to work up the nerve to tell him I had a problem. After all, the soloist is there to minister, not to have problems and be counseled. But after lunch one day, Dr. Brandt and I were still having coffee, and I timidly said, "You know, in this morning's session you were talking about being angry. You said some great things about temper, but I find sometimes I am so mad at my children I could scream." I was going to continue, but he stopped me with his I've-got-you-in-my-powerful-grip look and carefully (so I wouldn't miss it) said, "NOTHING can make you angry if you are filled with the spirit of love. On the other hand, ANYTHING can make you angry if you are filled with the spirit of hate and sin."

His words slammed into me like a two-by-four, and I really hurt, but it was a good hurt. He was right on target, and the truth of what he had said readily hit home. I felt the same kind of hurt you feel the moment a long, rough sliver is pulled out from under your festering fingernail. On the spot I asked God for my spirit of hate and sin to be controlled.

Then I did it again; I asked, "Tell me, Dr. Brandt, how long am I going to have to tell Laurie to make her bed every morning?" He hesitated for about a sixteenth of a second, leaned over, and about four inches from my face said matter-of-factly, "About fifteen or twenty years."

He then gave me three rules for Laurie and the bed bit, but I have used them over and over again for one situation after another; as Dick and I began using these guidelines, we started to really enjoy parenthood.

1. Set a rule or limit. (I had done that about making the bed: Make it each morning before school.)
2. See that the rule is carried out, and if you are not at home, see that someone else follows through on it. (Well, I'd done that, too.)
3. Give physical assistance to carry out the rule if necessary. (Now, I had NOT done that.)

The first morning I was home from the conference the old routine began. "Laurie, honey, have you made your bed yet?"

"No, mother, not yet, but I will."

Ten minutes later: "Laurie, did you make yo . . ."

"Just a second, mother." Etc., etc.

Finally I put my coffee cup down (now, THAT was really the hard part), took her by the hand, and said gently, "Come with me."

Suspiciously she asked, "Where are we going?"

"We are going to your room to make your bed, and I am going to help you because you need help."

I'll never forget the absolutely stunned look on her face as she shouted up at me, "I don't need any help at all!"

Quietly I said, "Oh, yes, you do. I've asked you several times if you had made your bed, and it seems to me you need my help to get it made." I was very calm and very filled with the spirit of love. I couldn't have lost my temper if I'd tried. Laurie was furious, and as we worked together I thought, *Who could help her make this bed with any more love than I, her mother? Who could train her, spank her, or discipline her with any more love than I, her mother?* Absolutely no one! No babysitter, no teacher, not even a grandma could be the mother that I could be.

After she left for school, I enjoyed another cup of coffee, and in an attitude of deep satisfaction, I realized I hadn't lost my temper and had definitely been patient.

I was delighted the next morning when I called to Laurie, "Honey, have you made . . ."

She interrupted, "Yes, I've already made my bed, and I DON'T need any help!"

We must never assume that once a rule is given, the child will automatically obey it; on the contrary, you MAY have twenty years of helping, but who can do it better than you?

After a few years of being a real Christian parent, I occasionally wished for another child so I could be, from conception, the kind of mother God had intended me to be to our first two. However, because we had almost lost Laurie with the RH factor problem, our doctors advised against having any more children. In the summer of 1964, while we were all sailing on Mission Bay in San Diego, the thought crossed my mind that the reason I was not enjoying this ride as I normally did was because I was not normal. "I think I'm pregnant," I said to Dick. The effect of my announcement caused Dick to momentarily lose his sailing ability, and we all came rather close to capsizing!

About a month later, both my doctors (who are brothers) confirmed what I already knew. I was slightly hysterical (and not with joy) as I recalled in detail Laurie's birth to one doctor, but he remained calm, took the first of what seemed like hundreds of tests and blood samples, and reassured me that the baby had an excellent chance of living. He was most confident. His brother was not, however, and a few months later he gently advised me to prepare myself because he felt the baby would not live.

On a typically hot, California day in September, as I left the doctor's air-conditioned office, his words really hit me. As I opened the outer door, I felt a double blast of heat. I was utterly crushed inside. Since I had missed those first all-important years with Laurie and Rick as a real mother, I desperately wanted another try at it. "God, please let me be worthy as a mother and let this baby live," I pleaded.

September melted into October and October blurred with pain into November. I had never been ill with either of the previous pregnancies, so I was totally unprepared to be so violently sick every moment. Each day I thought, *it couldn't get worse,* but each day it surprised me and managed to be more difficult.

My husband and children were love personified. Dick took over the management of the house, the washing, and the ironing, never once considering it beneath him as a man. He simply did it all out of his dear love for me; no task was too menial. I'll never forget his exasperated look the night he sat on the edge of my bed, while the children were setting the table for dinner, and he said, "Honey, what DO you do to hamburger patties to make them taste so good?"

Family and friends upheld me in prayer each day, and from the second week of November on, it was only by their prayers, thoughtfulness, and encouragement that I survived. There were only short periods of time each day when I did not have birth contractions and labor pains. Sometimes the pains were one hour apart, other times, barely six minutes. Never had I experienced anything like it. Pain robbed me of any ability to think or make clear decisions. Christmas came, and I tried to stay up for some of the day. But even dressed in a beautiful pale blue peignoir set (a lavish gift from Dick), I had to leave and go to our bedroom. I was sobbing with the intensity of the pain when I felt Dick's arms around me. He didn't say anything, but by non-verbal communication he told me he'd be there, he'd understand, and that my pain, my heartaches, and my sorrow were all his too. Thus armed, I stumbled through the next few days.

A couple of days after Christmas, standing in the family room of our home, with the beautiful afternoon sun filtering through the loosely woven drapes, everything was still and lovely, yet I knew I had to have an answer from God. I wept and sobbed as I stood there and reminded Him of His promise not to let us suffer more than we are able to bear. I was still standing there when the phone rang. It was the nurse from the specialist's office telling me to come in at nine the next morning.

The wretched corner of pain I had found myself in was the exact place of opportunity for which God had been waiting. He HAD to answer, and answer He did. As I look back on it, even though we so despise the corner experiences of our lives, that corner was the most thrilling corner I'd ever been backed into.

I saw the specialist, and that afternoon I was in the hospital with surgery set for late the following morning. I hadn't been in the bed five minutes when the first of seven ministers came to tell me hello, and they all prayed with me. The lady in the next bed desperately rang the emergency bell for the nurse. I heard her frantically ask, "Is the lady over there dying?"

"For pity sakes, no," answered the nurse.

"She must be," insisted the patient. "She hasn't been here ten minutes, and already seven ministers have prayed with her." I just laid there and smiled because most of our friends are in the ministry.

Late that night my condition changed and emergency surgery was arranged.

I have before me my account of that day, written some two weeks after surgery. It reads like this:

> It was two weeks ago today, early in the morning, that I was rushed through the hospital corridors, raced along dimly lit hallways, whisked downward in the elevator, past a nursing station, and into a sterile, green, operating room.

A room strange and cold, yet full of people working at frantic paces. I felt a little like the opening scene on a T.V. medical program.

There is something so terrifying about emergency surgery. No matter how strong you are in body and mind, and no matter how prepared you are spiritually, there is a naked fear which exposes every nerve so completely that you are left trembling violently and full of terror.

The baby was still moving within me, and my heart was full of thoughts, dreams, and hopes. *In spite of what they said, maybe he'll live — maybe this dear baby will live — oh, God, I hope so!*

As the physician steadied my body for the anesthetic, I began to say the 23rd psalm. I reached the second line, *"He maketh me to lie down in green pastures"* (this cold, hard operating table?), *"He leadeth me beside the still waters"* (these seven months of rushing, roaring rapids of pain?). *Well, it's just not true,* I reasoned. *Life is only a dry, barren desert — a dried up well of frustrations, fears, and pain. No "green pastures" or "still waters" . . .* Then my thoughts were interrupted, and I heard our baby son's first cry.

I left the dry, barren desert of pain and fear the moment the nurse showed me his dear little face. Our son, David. All the hope in the world soared and raced through every vein of my body — possibly all the suffering and pain had not been in vain! But hope was covered by a cloud — a cloud just big enough to cover my heart. I wondered if I had seen David for the last time here on earth. Mercifully, I was put to sleep.

In the fog of the next few hours, David continued to live, but I could only be bitterly realistic. Life really was a hot, barren, dry desert, arid and full of disappointments. Where were those "green pastures" or these "still waters"? Where?

Late that afternoon, my dear, weary, heartsick husband leaned over my bed, and as tenderly as I have ever heard him speak said, "Joyce, dear, the specialist is here, and it's all over. David is with the Lord." I reached up to touch his face, wet with his own sorrow, and in that instant we were suspended somewhere between that hospital room and the very Throne of God! The force of the presence of God was so overwhelming that it completely eclipsed the greatest moment of our sorrow. We could not pray; we could not even speak; the presence of God was so strong. We were being sustained by the prayers of hundreds of Christians, and the angels of God were there ministering to us! Thus, tenderly, did God begin to mend our broken hearts.

Tenderly, too, He began to show me that this barren experience was turning into the most enriching experience of my life. Now — now, when I really needed it, He did lay me down in green pastures, and suddenly I was resting in the peace of God beside the still waters of His love. From that dry, barren desert I was able to emerge fresh, vital, and anxious to once again be a wife to my husband, a mother to my children, and, in His name, a service of love and help to others.

In the days to follow there were more setbacks and more pain, yet as I lay there reading my Bible, I found I was able to say with the psalmist, "I shall not die, but live, and declare the works and recount the illustrious acts of the Lord" (Ps. 118:17, The Amplified Bible).

Early the morning of David's funeral (I was still in the hospital) I asked God for a special verse to carry me through the sadness of the day. I remembered that one of the visiting ministers had left a small book of treasured verses. I found it behind a flower vase on my bedside table and idly leafed through it.

I expected to find a verse of comfort or a verse about peace, but in His wisdom, He chose a verse not to lean on but to act on.

"This is the day which the Lord has brought about; we

will rejoice and be glad in it" (Ps. 118:24, The Amplified Bible).

The verse enabled me to turn loose the heart strings so lovingly attached to David and hand them willingly over to God for safekeeping.

When I was finally released from the hospital to spend four weeks in bed at home recovering, the countless acts of kindness by friends and loved ones swept into our home and over my body and soul like a fragrant perfume. Once more a healing took place.

A busy executive sent his secretary to my bedside. I taped a message to my radio listeners to somehow try and thank them for hundreds of letters and expressions of condolences. I told briefly on the tape about David; then near the end, in a weak, tired voice I said, "I have never experienced such physical pain, discouragement, and sorrow in all my life. At the same time, I have never experienced so much of God's love, His grace, and His comfort. Thank you from the depths of our hearts for your prayers." The letters continued and sustained us all.

One note came from my mother:

> My dearest,
>
> Though you have tears and sickness today, you stand a miracle of His loving grace.
>
> While you were in the hospital, the children behaved beautifully, and I'm sure outside of missing their home and dear parents, they were very happy and content with us and we loved having them — every minute of it. Dick looks so happy and relieved. Things are in God's hands and "He doeth all things well." My prayers and love for a wonderful new year ahead.
>
> Love, Mother.

A letter from Rev. Keith Korstjens sums up so many thoughts developed during those dark times when he said,

> Who knows how or in what wonderfully unexpected way God plans to use the present hardship? None can ever hope to fathom the magnificent plans of God! Yet, who has not seen Him take even the barest things of life and enshroud them with a rather startling honor and significance! I'm so glad we serve a God like that.
>
> Remember our love for you, and when the pain and discomfort are especially acute, remember, too, that He knows . . . oh, how well He knows. And someday we shall see the glory of this moment unfolded from the tapestries of God.

I held onto the truth of Keith's words because I knew, somehow, I would need them very much; I felt I was not through with grieving and that there would be more sorrow and more loss before too long.

One year after David's funeral, to the day, I rode in a funeral procession with my mother as her father was laid to rest in the arms of God. Less than nine months later I climbed into a long, black limousine again and began another funeral procession. And with great heartache and loss, we laid my mother to rest amid vivid pink roses, whispered our love, and promised to see her in *The Morning*.

Yes, I know someday we *shall* see the glory of those moments unfold from the tapestries of God, and we *shall* know it has been worth it all. We shall know, too, that we needed sorrow for the strength it builds. We need it like gold needs the refining process to be pure. And because of those tragic, grieving years, our lives have become strong and more like Him. Our hearts have become molded even more into His image, and as the song says, "Out of His infinite riches in Jesus, He giveth, and giveth, and giveth again!"

Through these losses I glimpsed a side of God I had never been privileged to see before, and this new view of God has enabled me to be capable of genuine compassion.

It also brought my appreciation of our other children into sharp focus. I looked at our children in a new light, and after David died, I dropped the phrase "My kids are driving me crazy" from my vocabulary. I thought about all the mothers in the world who would give just about anything to have their son or daughter back, tearing up the place and, in general, driving them crazy.

I would have loved it if the Lord had allowed David to stay with us, but since He didn't, I have set my heart on being the world's best mother to the two I do have. I don't always make it (especially on Mondays!), but I'm prepared to give it every ounce of strength, brains, and energy humanly possible.

The other night, dinner was dished in the plates, the candles lit, and everyone seated waiting for Dick. When he came in, he made some typical remark about the food on his plate, and we all laughed, especially me . . . even though his good-humored remark was carefully aimed at me. Rick roared with laughter; Laurie shook her head in mock disapproval and said, "Da---ddy!" I gave Dick my sternest look and hoped I could keep a straight face for one more second. It didn't work. For the millionth time, we started dinner with love, fun, and laughter. Finally, after we calmed down a bit, we reached out to hold each other's hands for prayer (a practice born for two reasons: the sense of touching hands is a lovely way of communicating love, and it does help to keep all hands out of the food during prayer). I doubt if I will ever forget that magnetic moment just before Dick began his prayer, as he looked at the children and said, "I pray when you marry a wife (he looked at Rick) and you marry a husband (then at Laurie) you will be as much in love as your mother and I."

The candlelight, the fragrant food, and the centerpiece of pink daisies; the sound of Dick's convictions and love ringing in his voice; the strong, firm hand of our sixteen-year-old Rick gripping mine; the sight of Laurie's fresh, four-teen-year-old beauty shining out from golden blond hair across the table . . . these sights and sounds are all engraved in pure gold on my memory forever. It was one of life's tenderest moments. I said to myself, "Oh, God, you've given me a second chance to really be a good mother. Help me not to misuse it."

On an album called "When Home Is Heaven" with Dr. Louis H. Evans, the topic of "Table Talk" is discussed. He describes our dinners (before we knew Christ) when he says:

"We go away from an empty plate with an empty heart. Let us not mix

> tea with tears
> coffee with correction
> soup with sourness
> salad with censoriousness
> corn with caustic
> anchovies with anger
> meat with dull monotony
> cuisine with quarreling."

Later he captures the feeling of the dinner I have just described, and many such dinners, since the Master has come to live with us.

> When the meal is over, let us push back our chairs with humble thankfulness, feeling that somehow Christ was our Guest and was pleased with the conversation; let us feel that we have added: fellowship to the feast, faith to the food, and vitality to the vitals; that love has covered the table as fine linen since man cannot live by bread alone; that He was heard to whisper, "I could make heaven out of such as these." Please be at our table, Lord.

The Lord is so much at our table that we have found reading devotions or the Bible after dinner has never been a contrived experience, but by gauging time spent and material covered to the ages of our children, it is always an exciting time. We've gone through many fine books and are presently on the Book of Proverbs from the *Living Psalms and Proverbs* paraphrase. It's only one chapter each night, but often it is one of our teen-agers who says, "Hey, don't stop there — go on," (although teen-agers are not noted for their ability to listen to Bible readings). The new translations communicate so well that the reading each night is quite lively. Speaking of communication, a much overworked word these days, this Book of Proverbs really makes a connection, like something we read just last night: "Don't talk so much. You keep putting your foot in your mouth. Be sensible and turn off the flow! When a good man speaks, he is worth listening to, but the words of fools are a dime a dozen" (Prov. 10:19, 20). Writing like that hardly leaves any room for our children to say, "I've read the Bible, but don't understand it." Even their parents can understand it.

Rarely are we formal at the devotions time, and we've encouraged our children to add comments or ask questions any time they care to; they often do, and we've found it to be a time of instruction, yet filled with gentle fun. The only time we really got hysterical was one night while we were still in Genesis; Dick was quietly reading along when Laurie yelled, "Hold it, dad, hold everything. What does circumcision mean?" Rick just slid under the table with a small groan. So much for the devotions.

Part of being parents is that business where daily, sometimes three times a day, you are called on to be lawyer, prosecuting attorney, judge, and jury all rolled in one. Making laws, handing down decisions, and distributing the sentences can drain the most vibrant of constitutions.

Some months ago, a violent movie showing crime in the raw was being seen by just "EVERYBODY!" I knew sooner or later I was going to be asked if our teen-agers could see it. Sure enough, both Rick and Laurie asked. The answer had to be "no" as far as Dick and I were concerned. We heard the familiar argument, "But everybody's going to see it," but we stuck to our guns. I did a considerable amount of research on the film and read all the reviews from the P.T.A. magazine to *Life*, and, based upon those findings, felt that the picture glamorized death, glorified sadistic violence, and no matter how artistically terrific it was (it won five Academy awards), seeing it would add nothing to the enrichment of our children's lives.

There were some who argued that the picture just showed life as it's really lived and that our children should know what's going on in the world around them and be "aware." Others said I shouldn't restrict my children like that — they were smart, and having a mind of their own, could judge for themselves as to how good the picture was AFTER they saw it.

127

I want our children to be aware of the big, bad, real world around them, but letting them see that movie was a little like telling them all about garbage and our sewage system. Should I tell them all the facts about garbage, lead them out to the trash cans and let them poke around, smell, and really get the feel of garbage for two hours and then ask them what they thought? And what honest mother and father would give their children boxes and boxes of candy, let them eat all they want, and let them grow up to decide whether or not they want the cavities? Dick and I went out on the limb (again) and took the risk — you know, the risk that your children might be violently opposed to your answer, and said, "No, our darlings, you may not go." I did not hear either one of them tell me how wonderful I was as a mother; in fact, they had a rather violent reaction in the opposite direction.

We have been learning, as parents, that there comes a time when we simply are not our children's friend, but rather their mother and father. There is quite a difference, but our children are certainly worth it all. They must be loved even in the lovely, yet awkward, immature stage; they must know we are proud of them even BEFORE they have achieved anything. We've learned, too, that with teen-agers you develop a great sense of humor or you become a hopeless neurotic!

Aside from the rules at our house, we have been learning something about companionship. Both Dick and myself have spent a considerable amount of time being with the children, individually and together as a family, to prepare them for leaving us. Sounds like a contradiction, but that's what we are doing with our children, and if, when they do go out into the world, they are unprepared for success or failure, guess who will get the blame? Mother and dad.

How can we really mold and shape our children to alert them to the pressures and tensions and joys of being an adult if we are never with them? It's not too easy with schedules and deadlines, but over and over again as I've asked God's wisdom, I've watched while a slip of time has opened up and a world of little memorable experiences called togetherness emerges.

Reading out loud to both children, teaching them to cook (and clean up the kitchen afterward), shopping trips, sailing trips, library trips, motorcycle rides, canoeing down the Colorado River, hiking up canyons near Mount Baldy, and riding surfboards at Laguna Beach are treasured times in our lives when we have been readying our children to leave us. From these experiences our children *catch* more than we will ever be able to *teach* them.

Looking back . . .

Once in awhile I have thought about all those years of being a selfish, neurotic, whining, self-pitying mother, and more often than not, a small but familiar voice has said: "You might as well face it: you failed during those years; you were a horrible mother. How could God ever really forgive you?"

Doubts and discouragement begin to rise, and I am tempted to do as the poem says, "Whip myself with remembered sins." But then I reread

Isaiah 44:22 and 55:7
Psalm 103:12

Micah 7:19
Jeremiah 31:34

and I say to my thoughts: "Satan, pack up your lying insinuations. I have accepted Christ's forgiveness by faith, and He (according to His Holy Word) remembers my sins no more!"

10

"Yes, Lord, let Your constant love surround us,
for our hopes are in You alone." Psalm 33:22

People ask God to change their marriage. They rarely
ask God to change themselves. How many times I asked
God to change all the conditions in our marriage during
those frantic five years. Never once did I ask Him to change
me. How pathetic, because God cannot change a marriage
until He changes the individuals.

As Dick and I look at our lives now, we realize that in
every area of living, God changed our thoughts, attitudes,
and goals. No area was left untouched by the matchless
hand of God.

I know now what it's like to laugh and love each other
all through dinner, to shoot glances of love and understanding above the heads of the children, saying in a thousand
little ways, "I love you" all evening. I know what it's like
to find a bag of chocolate-covered almonds (worth 38¢) on
my chair just before dinner. I know what it's like to be in
a crowded room talking intently to someone and then see
Dick across the room and read on his face, *Hey, you gor-
geous brunette, I love you,* or laugh at a wordless joke.
And I have seen his fierce look of pride when the last song

of my concert has ended, and later, over a dish of French onion soup, his look has said, *I'm so grateful to God for you.*

Dick has seen his ordinary lunch bag turn into a love-note-carrier. He has picked up his office phone to hear his wife say, "I know I saw you at breakfast, and I know I'll see you at dinner, but right now it's noon and I'm lonesome." He has asked for and received a white shirt or clean socks on any given day at any given time — now, that's a sign of TRUE love! While I take a considerable amount of teasing about the candles on our dinner table, Dick lights them anyway, and I've seen the reflected sparkle of love in his eyes.

The bedroom has now become for us the loving sanctuary in which an entire day of loving, caring, and understanding is culminated in the fullest expression ever known between a man and woman. Dr. Tim La Haye calls it, and rightly so, the marriage act — not the sex act.

I have watched God turn ordinary, incompatibly married people into extraordinary lovers, and I've known for some time now that only GOD could have thought the whole thing up and only GOD really knows how to teach two people the ways of loving.

One man heard me say this at a banquet, and afterward he said, "Boy, our marriage is like yours — my wife and I are completely incompatible. She's as different from me as day and night — the only thing we got goin' for us is Jesus." I thought, *Well, he might not have said that very poetically, but the point is very valuable. If all you "got goin' for you" is Jesus, you're a long way ahead of most marriages today.*

Learning God's way of loving has spilled over from our

bedroom to our family room with delightful effects on our children. Many a time after a verbal boxing round with Laurie over "Your bangs are too long," or "your skirt is too short," I've looked to Dick for help and then watched with proud joy as he has helped her take off her verbal fighting gear. It's done, incidently, by taking one hostile, fighting-mad little girl and gently enfolding her on one loving daddy's lap.

God transforms us, our marriage, and our children only after we really believe Him! Paul, in his letter to the Thessalonians, said, "And we will never stop thanking God for this: that when we preached to you, you didn't think of the words we spoke as being just our own, but you accepted what we said as the very Word of God — which, of course, it was — and it changed your lives when you believed it" (I Thess. 2:13). The key words in that verse are: "when you believed it."

By believing God's Word and really practicing it in daily living, the changes and the exchanges are truly miraculous. Husband and wife, mother and daughter, father and son, even community and job relations are sharply altered and changed by believing.

Remember the movie we wouldn't let our children see? Many months after the movie had moved on, while I was working some weeds over in the backyard with Rick, I asked him what he thought about that episode. He answered thoughtfully by saying, "Well, mom, I really wanted to see it because all my friends did, but I decided that if you and dad really didn't want us to go, well, more than wanting to see the picture, I wanted to obey you." I was so teary-eyed I could hardly tell the weeds from the flowers.

I did manage to say, "That's really very special, Rick. Did you know the Bible says that if you honor your mother and father, your days will be long and you'll really live a full life?"

He gave me a gigantic thirty-two-tooth smile, winked, and said, "I not only know about it, I'm counting on it!"

It is thrilling to be "believing" parents, but even more spectacular to find your children believing and experiencing God for themselves.

I'll never forget one experience with Laurie and Rick where God intervened and spoke directly to them. It happened one Sunday afternoon at Biola College. I was giving my complete testimony and was just about to tell the events of my suicide attempt, when I suddenly realized both children, now at an age where they would most certainly grasp all the horrible significance of my attempt, were sitting directly in front of me on the front row absorbing each word like a sponge.

Oh, God, I thought, *what will they think? How will they respect me if they know the awful truth? Will they think less of me because I tried to kill myself?*

Instantly I was fortified with God's unexplainable peace, and I released the grip on my panic, swallowed hard, and finished my story.

The children were the first to reach me after the concert. *Oh, God,* I panicked, *please give me the right answers for them. Please prepare my heart!*

I shouldn't have worried; God loves our children more than we do, and we always forget the completeness of His caring.

Both children, in different words but with the same meaning, said, "Oh, mother, we are so glad you and daddy didn't get a divorce, and we are so happy we are a family!"

Even now, as I recall that moment, I can still feel the surge of thankfulness in my heart. The children heard the suicide part, accepted it, and grasped the most important issue: that God had, by His stubborn love, united us as a family. The proof of the believing had been in actually living day by day as a happy family, and God so sweetly put the emphasis on the right spot.

I am continually asked how being a wife, mother, singer, writer, and broadcaster, all fit together, and my only answer is that they do. It takes evaluating schedules periodically, it takes long talks with Dick, and it takes much prayer time, but it all does work out. The only time I mess up is when, for some dumb reason, I reverse the order of wife, mother, and singer, or even switch the order. These rules of life are the ones I know God wants for the Landorf family. This may not be true for you, but scripturally — for a woman — the husband is to be the head of the home, the children secondary, and all the other pieces of life after that.

Following the road Christ points out to you may not be easy — who said it would be? Even our Lord said, "In the world you will find trouble," but *as you travel* you'll know it's worth it (John 16:33, *The Twentieth Century New Testament*, Moody Press: Chicago). Robert Frost wrote of being a traveler and said,

> Two roads diverged in a wood, and I —
> I took the one less traveled by,
> And that has made all the difference.

If the stubborn love of God had not pursued us, we would have missed this less traveled road. We would have missed big things like living in peace with each other and loving together, but we also would have missed some small, gentle joys like cooking and sewing, walking on warm, sunny beaches, and listening to bright bits of dialogue from our growing children.

I would have missed a remark by Laurie the other night and THAT would have been a loss. I was tired from a long day of taping radio programs, and Laurie asked me how many programs I'd finished. "Twelve, today," I said. That was over two weeks of programs, and the fatigue I felt was lining my face with pale weariness.

She skipped off down the hall and called back, "That's too bad, mother; you need your eagle."

She was already tucked into bed ten minutes later when I finally HEARD what she said. I switched on her light . . . "Did you say eagle? What eagle?" I asked.

"Oh, you know, daddy's your eagle," she explained.

"Honey, I don't have the remotest idea of what you are talking about."

She patiently sat up in bed. She didn't look like any intellectual philosopher with those pink and yellow curlers in her hair, but she had grasped the depth of the love between her mother and father and had sensed that the road we had chosen to travel had, indeed, made the difference!

"Daddy," she continued, "is your own private eagle. He's big and strong, and when you are very tired he spreads open his big wings, calls to you, and then he folds those big, feathery wings around you and it's all right. It's so warm and nice in his wings that you just snuggle up and go to sleep. He's your eagle."

"My darling, you are absolutely right," was all I could manage before I kissed her good night.

Sometimes when I'm tired of being a wife, a mother, a PTA board member, a Sunday school teacher, and a member of the choir (and I *do* get tired just like you do), I think of moments like the one with Laurie and somehow the boredom and fatigue melt away. Ask any widow if all the energy expended for her husband was worth it, and she'll tell you in no uncertain terms that it was. Ask any mother who has lost a child if she would be willing to get tired and bored for the sake of her child, and her "yes" will resound around the world. But to have missed all this . . . that would have been the tragedy. I could have traveled the wrong road forever. Oh, dear Lord, what an awful thought. . . .

Less than two months ago the local newspaper ran a short article about the greyhound race in Portland, Oregon. It said that nine dogs had just learned the awful truth about the rabbit they chase each racing night — it was made out of tin! A cat had entered the tin rabbit's housing unit and bent the bunny's supporting arm. At the first turn on the track, the rabbit started sparking and slowing down; then, just before the final stretch, he gave up and the dogs finally caught him. The article ended by saying, "The race was over. All money bet was refunded. And nine bewildered dogs went back to their kennels."

As I read that, I almost spilled my coffee laughing so hard. I'd always wondered what the dogs would do if they ever caught the rabbit.

Running races after metallic rabbits . . . I stopped laughing and recalled all the running, scrambling, stumbling races I'd run — and to catch what? A tin, fake, non-existent rabbit, an elusive dream, an invisible hope, an endless race going absolutely nowhere and lasting — forever? Yes, that's an accurate description of my chaotic, pell-mell existence. Then there came the day when somehow, because I was getting nowhere, I changed direction and the tin rabbits of my life began to chase me. I was aware that I was being pursued, and I tried to run faster. I tried to hide, to disappear, but it was to no avail. God finally crushed me into breathless surrender and I gasped, "Yes, Lord, Yes!" From that moment on, I was possessed by Him. No more chasing, no more stumbling, and no more futile races.

I really wish the Lord could have won me without the chasing and that final agonizing blow on the head before He could capture my attention; but for some of us, stubborn as we are, that's what it takes. One translation of Isaiah 30:18 says, "He will conquer you to bless you." When I first read that I thought, *Well, I WISH that could have been avoided, but if I had to go through all those years of agony and even try to take my life so that I could be conquered by Him, it was worth every, single, horrible second of it!*

I wonder, too, why did God choose me? Not only choose me, but capture me? I doubt if there is a day that passes without my questioning Him with, "Why me?"

But winging past the portals of heaven, and rushing beyond the gates of splendor, I hear words from the very heart of God:

"My child, I HAVE chosen you . . . I've pursued you

to the extreme edge of the world. I caught you between the earth and sky. I seized you and tenderly brought you back. You had all but vanished. You were almost gone, but I, because I love you, breathed into you once more the breath of life and you will live. You'll live not only for this brief span of time on earth, but forever and ever!"

Oh, love that would not let me go! Stubborn, stubborn love!

EPILOGUE

"He has given me a new song to sing, of praises
to our God. Now many will hear of the glorious
things He did for me, and stand in awe before the
Lord, and put their trust in Him."   Psalm 40:3

I first told this story of God's stubborn love in public
several years after the day of the lifesaving phone call.

I had been asked to sing and speak for the Hollywood
Christian group. My audience was made up of men and
women connected, in some way, with the entertainment in-
dustry. As I began telling them about some of the daily
miracles God was doing, I realized I should tell them about
my actual conversion. So, for the first time publicly, I told
of those agonizing days. When I reached the part about
the suicide, I happened to look at Dick. Something terrible
was taking place inside him, and as I watched, his face
mirrored the agony of his heart.

When I finished, everyone moved into an adjoining room
for coffee, but I waited for Dick. He was very quiet. I
knew his thoughts would form into words, and in a few
moments he said:

"Joyce, you can't tell this story of ours in public. You
just can't! I relive each moment as you tell it. It's too
hard to hear. I feel like I'm being torn apart." The words

poured out quietly but intently until we were interrupted by two very young, very beautiful, very disturbed people. Both were crying, but he spoke first.

"We are where you two were." His tone was desperate.

She interrupted, "We've tried everything. Nothing works. We can't go on — we've both considered suicide, and until tonight we were sure there was no other answer. We want to do what you did. Will you help us?".

The next minutes were the most meaningful and thought-provoking moments of our life. We prayed for these two precious people. Then it was their turn, and as they prayed, we watched and listened as they confessed their sins and needs to God. A miracle took place before our astounded eyes.

He stood taller, and she looked more beautiful. The tensions ebbed from their faces, and the first, sweet fragrance of God's forgiveness began sweeping over their souls. They turned to each other, each talking, asking forgiveness of the other, laughing and crying at the same time. And as they did, they took on the most radiant glow we had ever seen.

Later that night, as we walked slowly and quietly toward our car, Dick stopped, put his arm around my shoulder, and said, "Joyce, if God can use the most hellish time of our life to work the fantastic miracle we just witnessed in the lives of those two people, you *must* tell it again and again."

So time and time again we have shared our story, no, more accurately, we've *given* it away and have seen faces transformed by the sudden awareness of Him — the wide-open, surprised expression as people say, "God really cares for me. He really does!" We also understand a little more clearly what Jesus meant when He told us that if we found our life we would lose it, but if we lost it for His sake, we would find it. In giving our faith away, our own lives have become more abundant, more joyous, and more *alive*.

It occurs to me as I finish these pages that I might have overlooked something very important. Maybe you are teetering on the extreme edge of living, and tears of frustration, worry, and anger are bathing your daily existence. Perhaps right now you are thinking, *Oh, Joyce, I'm right where you were. I'm there today, right now. Do I really dare hope for God's miracle in my life? Can God reach down, forgive my sins, and then heal all my diseases? Can He make anything out of my life when there's so little left?*

And I must tell you: "Yes! Yes!" I have lived through this before. For several years now I have put it to the test. I have felt Him write down the answers to life with His own fingers across the walls of my heart. If I could reach out of these pages, I would grab you by the shoulders and say, *"He can be trusted!* He really can be trusted! He's the same yesterday, today, and forever! Trust Him!"

Then I would take your hand and run with you to the very throne of God and shout, "Oh, God, dear, Almighty God, do it for her as you did for me. Do it for him as you did for Dick. Do it for their children as you did for our children!"

Then God's powerful voice would boom back like a thundering cannon to you. "Give me your sins, your longings, your griefs, and your needs — my Son has already paid the price. Your debt is free and clear. I shall replace the agony with ecstasy, the sorrow with singing, the fears with faith, but first give me your sins."

Then I would stand back, because it would be up to you. When He holds out the choice of life — victorious life — to you, I can't reach out and grab it for you. You must make the move yourself.

You might hesitate and say, "I'm afraid; I have tried before and I have so many questions, so many doubts."

But before I could answer, something would make you look up, and when your eyes really met His, you'd see His look of love. His compassion would surround you and you'd breathe, in total surrender.

"Yes, Lord, yes. I cannot resist you. I have rebelled. I have done things my own way — but I cannot reject your look of love."

God's forgiveness would penetrate your mind, your heart, and your will. The first sweet winds of peace would gently cool your face.

Then we would leave His glorious presence and come back.

We would come back to the street where you live, the house where you eat and sleep, the life where you work and love. We would come back to the contemporary world of now, and you'd begin a most fantastic experience.

You would find you not only believe on Christ, but you could follow Him. You would not only know His miracle of forgiveness, but you could mature and grow in the daily press of mundane things, and then you could say with David the psalmist,

> Let us praise the Lord together, and exalt His name.
> For I cried to Him and and He answered me! He freed
> me from all my fears. . . .
> Yes, the Lord hears the good man when he calls to Him
> for help, and saves him out of all his troubles.

The Lord is close to those whose hearts are breaking . . .
The good man does not escape all troubles — he has them
too. But the Lord helps him in each and every one.
God even protects him from accidents. . . .
But as for those who serve the Lord, He will redeem them;
everyone who takes refuge in Him will be freely par-
doned (Ps. 34:3, 4, 17-20 and 22).

You see, God can be trusted; and you can know real
living, for His love is very stubborn.